The Power of Family Vision

The Power of Family Vision

Choosing to be Intentional will Change your Family and the Generations to Come

Bill and Danielle Ford

Visit http://www.c2family.com

Edited by David Hughes, http://davidhugheswriter.com/

Printed in the United States of America.

ISBN-13: 9781505422078
ISBN-10: 1505422078

Abstract

Bill and Danielle share insight on the supernatural power of the family and how a vision statement can launch your family into the destiny God intended.

Dedication

This book is dedicated to our children, who also wanted more. Without saying a word, they asked us to lead them and be examples of real Godly fruit for our family. They stepped out with us in faith, played their unique and important roles, got involved, encouraged us, and, most important, became the evidence of what God promised one long morning in our backyard.

Our five kids are world changers, and their kids will be also. Thank you, Lord, for giving us a vision, the courage, and the double portions of faith it took to persevere. Now we ask for a multiplication in every family who reads this book.

In Jesus's name.

Introduction

In 2009 we found ourselves in the proverbial desert: parched, hungry, and lost. We had lost our way. The promised land of material success and the American Dream was only a mirage. We had worked so hard to get to a place of worldly success, only to find that most of what we believed in was a lie.

Our American Dream was to work hard, save money, acquire stuff, and retire well. That was it—our dream and destiny were to enjoy all the fruits of our labor and do whatever we wanted, whenever we wanted. What we began to realize, almost too late, was that this place was a desert where no amount of water could quench the thirst stemming from a lack of real meaning and significance for us and our family.

We lacked the most important element in this definition of success: true vision. Not our vision, but God's vision for our family. God knew what was right for us—and knows for you—that we were created for a greater purpose, a greater story, and a destiny that would fill both heart and spirit with true joy and peace. Nothing else in the world can provide this, no matter how hard we work or how much we save. There's more. Much more.

There is power in vision. Every successful businessman or woman knows this. They have all written a clear vision statement to clarify what success means as defined by their industry, a vision of achievement by a worldly standard. What if a vision for you and your family changed everything? Especially the things that really matter: your family, your marriage, and your children in this generation and for generations to come? There is power here, power for everything and everyone that matters to you. It will change how you define success, and it will change the outcome for your life.

Why did we write this book? Because family matters, and the power of family vision leads families to reap the greatest rewards God has prepared for them.

Your family, your marriage, your children, and your God-given destiny matter. Do you want to change the outcome? Do you want more? If you do, read on.

In order to have more, you must first want more. God has so much more for you right now, and His vision for you is powerful. This power, properly harnessed, will manifest to overcome obstacles, take authority, and change many lives forever. Most important, this power will change *you*, your family, and the generations that follow.

By the way, it's never too late. As we share our redemption story, you will realize that God can use everything you have already done to bring about His greatest reward for your family.

Blessings to you and your new supernatural family,

Bill and Danielle Ford

Table of Contents

Authors' Note

The Power of Family Vision was written as a result of the victory wrought in our family through the grace of God. Danielle and I as a couple have worked through every page, exercise, and scripture verse with intentionality and commitment. We desire you to do the same.

This book is a result of a real battle we fought for our family and a testimony to God's redemption, supernatural power, and the abundant love He always intended for us. We experienced many victories as we obediently followed the process the Lord, through the Holy Spirit, laid before us. We have notebooks full of the very truths, principles, and exercises that we share in the following chapters. To provide a way for you to have the same experience and victory for your family, we composed an accompanying workbook that will become a keepsake for your family as generations look back into the past to acknowledge your courage to fight for their future and see the evidence of the fruit of your labors.

The workbook is designed to complement this book and offer you a strategic place to chronicle your thoughts, dreams, and the tangible steps you take to create the legacy and vision for your family as God reveals them to you. If you do not already have the workbook, you may order it from www.c2family.com. You will be prompted throughout this book to turn to the workbook for more explanation of the steps, examples of how to create your vision, and as a place to document your progress into the supernatural power of a family vision. You will know when to turn to the accompanying workbook when you see this:

Reflection: Please turn to the accompanying workbook before you move on.

Foreword

Let us encourage you: your family matters and this book will change things.

When we read books, go to hear a speaker or listen to a sermon they are typically either inspirational or practical. We end up either inspired with no direction or we know exactly how to take action but have not been inspired to do so. Rarely do we find a resource that is both inspirational and practical.

That is why we are so excited about this book! It both inspires us to want more for our family and it's also a 'Take It Home And Do It' step by step resource! *The Power of Family Vision* provides a practical game plan to help you lead your family and give you clear direction so you can stay focused on the prize! 1 Corinthians 9:24 states, 'Do you not know that in a race all the runners run, but only one gets the prize? Run in such a way to get the prize!' This book is your 'SUCH A WAY'! It's the 'HOW TO'! You really can **'TAKE IT HOME AND DO IT'!** No need to flounder around as a parent and think you can quote a few verses now and then and take your kids to church and hope that something sticks.

Do you really want meaningful connection with your children and your spouse so that you can operate as a family unit and discover God's masterful plan for YOUR unique family? This book and workbook give you the vision to 'see' what that looks like in your family. Bill and Danielle are like encouraging coaches as they warn you of possible obstacles and encourage you to press on to the goal! They have earned their 'you can do it' attitude because they have walked through it themselves and have seen their family redeemed and transformed. So get on board and know that when God says **ALL THINGS ARE POSSIBLE WITH HIM,** He not only means it, He has provided the way to accomplish it. Bill and Danielle offered to be His hands and feet through this well thought out resource.

2 Chronicles 16:9 tells us that the Lord looks to and fro throughout the earth that He may strongly support those whose heart is completely His. The Fords decided to be that family and **your family can also be that family.** When you factor in the multiplication plan laid out in *The Power Of Family Vision* resources, it is actually possible to see how one's family, community, city, nation, and even the world can be changed. So as the optimist always says, 'Let's do this'! Or, as Bill and Danielle say, "**C2it!**"

Phil and Skissy Caldwell
Intentional Parents and
Grandparents from Texas

One

Recapture the Dream

THE DREAM

Four-year-old Callaway climbed onto a trampoline that had been transformed into a rodeo chute before his very eyes. His goal: ride a bull everyone knew as Punisher. The bull snorted and pawed the dirt on the arena floor like the beast he was. Well, Punisher was really Callaway's ten-year-old brother Tucker, but for the next eight seconds he would turn into a two-ton Brahma bull who wanted to toss this cowboy into the next county. Callaway's glove was tightly taped to his hand, and his chaps were belted around his waist. His heart pounded with anticipation. He was going to be the first. So far, no other kid in the neighborhood had been able to ride this bull for the full eight seconds.

Callaway saw that the bullfighter was in place and ready, waiting for the gate to swing open. The little bull rider took a breath, eager to embark on the quest of his life. He had been dreaming and preparing for this moment his entire life. There was no turning back. The dream was about to become real.

The fans waited quietly as the gate handler watched for the go signal. The bull rider's head nodded. The gate opened. Callaway spurred and kicked; his right hand waved as his left hand gripped the bull rope tightly. The bull bucked out of the gate and twirled to the right, just as the cowboy knew he would. He needed to hold on for what might be the longest eight seconds of his life.

When the horn blasted he was still on top. The victor. He released his grip and bounced to the ground to receive his applause. But the show was not yet over. With one last dash, Punisher took aim to take revenge on Callaway. The bullfighter rushed to the rescue as the crowd roared. It was epic. An adventure the bull, the boy, the bullfighter, and the crowd would not soon forget. Until tomorrow, of course, when it would all be played out again with a new bull, a new rider, and the next backyard adventure.

This was the scene from our daughter's kitchen window as we watched our grandchildren live out their imaginary dream. What struck us both was how real it was for them. Day after day their adventure was real and even today our grandson, Callaway, lives for the day this dream becomes real. He feels destined to be a bull rider like his father.

Do you remember the dreams you had as a child? If you were a boy, you most likely dreamed about saving the world through some great adventure of your own. In your heart and mind this adventure was quite real; you may have even dressed the part. You may have worn a cape and donned a sword, or you went deep undercover to carry out your mission. You used words like "Charge!"

"Attack!" or "All for one, and one for all!" This adventure was so important that you convinced your friends to play a role to achieve your objective of saving the world. The more real you made it, the more others wanted to join in.

If you were a girl, your adventure may have been about saving the world as well, but most likely you were also raising children and had horses to take care of while you were doing it. Your adventure included a hero who arrived to rescue you from the monotonous and the mundane, and he became a partner in this epic story. You may have also equipped yourself with a sword and keen senses to fight the battle to help your hero succeed in this most honorable objective. The best part was that you were not just wanted, but needed. The dream brought you life and purpose. The whole idea of the adventure made your heart pound with anticipation. You were made for this! Your girlfriends watched in awe as you lived out this exciting make-believe life while you fulfilled your purpose, and in your heart you knew that one day this was going to become your reality. Once you got just a little older, nothing was going to stop you. Nothing.

So what happened? Did you do it? Did you accomplish the vision you had for your life and your family? Did you save the world? Did you ride the bull? What stopped you?

THE DREAM FORGOTTEN

Most dads and moms we talk with tell us with a sigh, "No, it didn't happen." The dreams and the visions got lost in the day-to-day reality of school, work, raising children, and chasing the American Dream. Some tell us they don't even know what happened. One day they woke up and found themselves forty or fifty years old, with so many things going on they didn't even have time to dream anymore. They regret not having lived out the dream, or they feel guilty that they are not living a life of true adventure or experiencing a real courageous life that truly matters. Not only did they not save the world, they're not sure they changed a single thing. What they ended up with were house payments, credit card debt, kids' school expenses, car payments, and a few trips every year to try to get some perspective. They attempt to convince themselves and those around them that they really are happy and have achieved some significance.

Please don't misunderstand us—there is nothing wrong with success and having things. In fact, it's the heart and character of God to give and bless with abundance, but when the focus is on the stuff and not on the destiny God has for us, we end up with a whole bunch of things and not enough adventure. Many of us, as we get older, feel like we have missed something. In fact, there is a palpable sense that something was meant to happen, but didn't.

We know this all too well. We found ourselves living the American Dream. We had a nice home and nice cars, and we took nice trips mostly because we thought we deserved it. That was the story of our lives. We went to church and gave to the needy, but outside of that our lives didn't produce much fruit, not the fruit that mattered, anyway—the fruit meant to fulfill our very souls. The purpose we were created to fulfill and the mission to make our hearts come fully alive had been lost somewhere along the way. But perhaps it had not really been lost. Perhaps we had just believed a lie, and had not realized that God had so much more for our family and for us. Perhaps it was not too late.

The lie we bought into was that our life was all about us. We were trying to fill a worldly definition of significance. We wanted to prove to the world that we were successful by its standards, and this was never part of the dream. As we look back now, there was nothing world changing or significant in what we were chasing. God's purpose and vision for our family were so much bigger.

One potential tragedy of our story was what we were teaching our children: they saw our worldly success and the things we accumulated. We had coveted the lifestyle we achieved, and we wanted others to covet it as well. It was a trap and a lie. But isn't that what we are taught? To build a career, have children, make money, and save for retirement? The truth is, we were lost, and we were teaching our children by our example to strive for the same life of spiritual insignificance. We lived in the desert of irrelevance. If we had put a match to every material and superficial thing in our lives, there would not have been much left.

We were among hundreds who showed up to church on Sunday and consumed the message, but nothing really changed. We were hearers of the Word but not really doers. We took what we wanted but never applied the real truth, even in our home. In the book of James, the writer tells us that in order to produce fruit we must be doers and not just hearers of God's Word. In simple terms, only listening to God's truth without applying what we hear brings no change, no power, and no abundance.

> But be doers of the Word [obey the message], and not merely listeners to it, betraying yourselves [into deception by reasoning contrary to the Truth]. (James 1:22, *AMP*)

We knew Jesus, but we can't truthfully say we were His disciples, nor were we teaching our kids to be His disciples. The reality of the situation at the time was that we were not a great positive influence on our children. Not that we were bad parents, but because we were not intentional in the discipleship of our children, we were leaving so much to chance.

The truth we must realize as parents is that, with or without our intentionality, our kids are being influenced by something or someone. In fact, an all-out war is being waged against our children and grandchildren. Although it is an extremely subtle war, if we do not become intentional and train our children to seek God's greatest rewards, they will quickly settle for the rewards of the world. Many of life's rewards are not corrupt in themselves, but settling for material affluence and self absorption will ultimately leave you and your children unfulfilled.

THE INFLUENCES

Where do these influences originate? They come from several areas that have captured the attention of our children, such as social media, music, and every electronic device in our homes. They even come through individuals in whom we have entrusted our children's care, such as teachers, coaches, and friends. Some of these people tell them they need to have things, they deserve it, and that it really is all about them. These influences spur our kids to question their faith as they are attacked with contrary moral messages designed to change their minds.

One evening during dinner, our son Noah, who was fourteen at the time, told a story about a debate he had gotten into with one of his teachers. Noah likes to debate issues, sometimes just for fun, to find out what others believe and, in some way, to confirm his own beliefs, but as he told this story we heard something different in his voice.

Noah had debated his teacher over a cultural and moral issue, and they clearly stood on opposite sides of the argument. The teacher, who was there to teach and influence our son, had an opinion on a subject with which our son didn't agree, and Noah was not going to relent. As I listened to his story, I realized by his tone that he had questions he had not asked directly. When Noah finished, he looked straight at me. In that moment I realized his unspoken questions were, "Dad, I just debated my teacher over a cultural and moral issue. Was that okay? Wasn't she supposed to be the authority? Was I supposed to agree with what she was teaching?"

The next question was the most important one. When Noah finished the story, I realized the question he was silently asking me was, "Dad, I'm not sure now what I really believe. Will you help me?" Wow! The teacher's firm but inaccurate position was nothing short of an attack against one of our kids. It made Danielle and me angry, but, most important, it brought to light the battle we were fighting. That evening's discussion became a pivotal point on our journey to becoming intentional parents, and the experience moved us one step closer to the destiny God had for us in encouraging other parents to do likewise.

At one of our conferences, while parents shared with one another about how their kids were being influenced, one dad painted a vivid picture of how out of control his home had become, and how hopeless he felt. He described his household as a bunch of separate apartments where everyone holed up in their rooms and lived their individual lives with their TVs, phones, computers, and music. He knew almost nothing about what they were seeing or hearing, and even less about how it was influencing them. He felt overwhelmed.

We encounter overwhelmed parents at many of our events. The anger and frustration that was first felt when they realized they were losing the battle wanes to confusion, sometimes denial, then the wave of defeat that leads to becoming overwhelmed. Sometimes it is for good reason that we, as parents, become overwhelmed. Until we realize the real threat, we are seldom moved to take action against it, so we allow the battle to get the best of us.

When we first recognized the war being waged against our family, we felt we were also losing the battle. It was absolutely devastating. Fear and hopelessness overwhelmed us as well. The enemy was having his way with our family, and we had allowed it. We felt the world was having a greater impact on our children than we were. It was a scary moment of revelation for us, but as the reality of the situation sunk in, it gave us a reason to enter the battle. We were ready to fight for our children, and fight we did, with everything we had.

We had to ask ourselves some tough questions: What happened? How did we get here, and what were we going to do about it? We were sure of one thing: we weren't ready or equipped to fight this battle on our own. We needed help—supernatural help.

Our story is one of redemption. God has supernaturally taken our family to the place we now find ourselves only through receiving His vision, His power, His love, and His leadership. We now see real fruit in our home and our children. Because of our journey, we want to encourage you that, although the battle is not easily won, it is a battle worth fighting. With the right tools and encouragement, you will succeed. The pages that follow will equip you, give you hope, and a successful plan. Your story can become a redemption story as well. No matter where you are in this battle, you can overcome. Our message is not about perfect parents raising perfect kids; it's about intentional parents raising intentional kids. Dream big for your family, and be strong and courageous. Be intentional.

WHAT'S AT STAKE

What's at stake is the very nature and identity of family as created by our Maker. The family is being redefined through the lies and influences of the world, and this attack is specifically being waged on our children. Most of us can clearly recognize it. You know it's happening, and maybe you feel helpless to do anything about it. As this attack continues, we try to protect our families in every way we can. As parents, we care most about protecting our children's hearts because it is their hearts that will determine the course of their lives.

SATAN WANTS OUR CHILDREN BECAUSE HE WANTS THEIR FUTURE.

What's at stake is the next generation, and the generations that follow. The world is inundating our children with moral messages every hour of every day, and most of us don't agree with these messages. These messages carry an agenda of moral and cultural ideology that goes against what we are trying to teach our kids. It's a war; make no mistake about it, but know this: it's a war we can and must win. There is too much at stake for our families and the next generations.

The war is very real. You find casualties as close as your last holiday gathering. When we just look at the families around us, we see more of the image from the hit tv series, *Modern Family,* than real supernatural fruit and abundance. The devastation is evidenced by families who lack the courage or even the understanding to believe and know in their hearts that God created their family for a supernatural purpose. To paraphrase Proverbs 29:18, families lack a vision; and their children and grandchildren are perishing.

Families matter to our Creator. He has a unique vision for each of them, and throughout the next chapters of this book we will encourage you to receive and live out the vision He has for you and your family; a vision that will result in real change.

REMEMBER THE DREAM

Now allow yourself to go back to your dream. What was—or is—the dream God planted in your heart? Do you remember it? Do you know what it is? Can you write it down? Can you speak it? Allow the Holy Spirit right now to remind you of what it was and what your life should be. Make no mistake—God created you and your family for a purpose, and the Holy Spirit wants to lead you into all truth (John 16:15) and into this adventure of a lifetime. The purpose of this book and the accompanying workbook is to provide the guidance to define the vision for you and your family and change the outcome for your children and grandchildren.

Read the verse below. Remember, God is with each of us, and He wants to walk and talk with us throughout our day and in every area of our lives. He guides us through His Spirit, who resides in each one of us. If you feel like He's not communicating with you right now, take time to listen to your heart about your life and the vision for your future. Believe this: He wants you to live out this dream for yourself and for your family.

> But when He, the Spirit of Truth (the Truth-giving Spirit) comes, He will guide you into all the Truth (the whole, full Truth). For He will not speak His own message [on His own authority]; but He will tell whatever He hears [from the Father; He will give the message that has been given to Him], and He will announce and declare to you the things that are to come [that will happen in the future]. (John 16:13, *AMP*)

THE DREAM OF SIGNIFICANCE

In her book *The Top Five Regrets of the Dying*, Bronnie Ware tells the story of how she found herself tending to the needs of those in their last days of life. As she listened to their stories she began to blog about what her patients shared of what they wished they had done differently. It was not surprising that no one wished they had made more money, had a bigger house, or worked longer or harder. Every story contained deep emotions about how they wished they had lived more, laughed more, had deeper relationships with others, and had more courage to truly make a difference. Ware wrote:

> The lack of courage was the most common regret of all. When people realize that their life is almost over and look back clearly on it, it is easy to see how many dreams have gone unfulfilled. Most people had not honored even half of their dreams and had to die knowing that it was due to choices they had made, or not made. Health brings a freedom very few realize, until they no longer have it. (2012, p. 37)

BE COURAGEOUS

Is this why the Lord encourages us throughout Scripture to be strong and courageous? Look at the story in the first chapter of Joshua. There is a crisis happening in the desert. Moses has died. The Israelites are leaderless. So what does God do? He chooses a new leader. He tells Joshua in verse 2 to arise and take Moses's place to accomplish the promise He had made through Abraham and Moses to enter the Promised Land and live in abundance.

This was a game changer for Joshua; God chooses him to fulfill the destiny of the Israelite people. How is he going to do this on his own? Well, he's not. God first gives Joshua the vision in Chapter 1: 3–5 (*AMP*). There, God tells Joshua,

> 3 Every place upon which the sole of your foot shall tread, that have I given to you, as I promised Moses.
> 4 From the wilderness and this Lebanon to the great river Euphrates—all the land of the Hittites [Canaan]—and to the Great [Mediterranean] Sea on the west shall be your territory.
> 5 No man shall be able to stand before you all the days of your life. As I was with Moses, so I will be with you; I will not fail you or forsake you.

Wow, now that's a vision. God commissions Joshua to lead the Israelite people into the Promised Land. Can you see this picture vividly in your mind as God describes the vastness of what Joshua is going to do? How is he going to do it? God helps him by taking him from the vision to the action steps needed. First, three times God tells him to have courage. In verse 6 (*AMP*) He tells Joshua,

> 6 Be strong (confident) and of good courage, for you shall cause this people to inherit the land which I swore to their fathers to give them.

In verse 7 (*AMP*) He tells him again.

> 7 Only you be strong and very courageous, that you may do according to all the law which Moses My servant

> commanded you. Turn not from it to the right hand or to the left, that you may prosper wherever you go.

Again, in verse 9 (*AMP*), it is not just encouragement; God commands Joshua that in order to fulfill His vision and destiny he must be courageous.

> 9 Have not I commanded you? Be strong, vigorous, and very courageous. Be not afraid, neither be dismayed, for the Lord your God is with you wherever you go.

Why do so many people go through their entire lives and not live out their vision? It's a matter of courage. Not courage that comes from the natural realm, but courage originating from the Lord himself; the supernatural realm. It's a belief and a faith that God will provide you with everything you need to accomplish His vision for your family.

Like Joshua, you and I were created to dream and live out our dreams to fulfill something greater than we could ever do in the natural realm. We must first know and trust that the Lord will be with us and give us everything we need in order to fulfill it, especially courage.

As children, it is easy to dream. We have our whole lives ahead of us, so we believe we can do anything. As we grow older things get in the way; we start to believe it less, and we don't dream as often, if at all. That doesn't have to and shouldn't be the case. God created you to dream, have visions, and do more than you think you can in your life. With His supernatural help, you and your family will be fully alive as you fulfill your calling and purpose. These things start with a vision—dream big for your family. Why? Because there's more. Believe it.

When Danielle and I work with families individually or through our conferences, we ask our participants to do something a little creative and sometimes uncomfortable. We ask them to close their eyes, get out of the here and now, and receive a big vision. We ask them to seek a vision of more for their family, a vision of abundance, destiny, doing something that matters, a vision of true significance. We ask you to do the same at the end of this chapter.

What we would ask them is: If time and money were no object, what would you be doing? How would your spouse be involved? How about the kids? Who else might be involved? Who would it impact, and why would it matter if you accomplished it? Some families immediately begin to draw and articulate the dream. Others need more time. This is where we pray and ask God for revelation for each family because we know you were created for a purpose, and He wants to help you discover and fulfill it.

Recently, while having coffee with a dad, he told me that the vision he has for his family lasts far beyond his life and this generation. "It's a multigenerational vision."

"Wow," I said, "now that's big, but not too big for God." I loved hearing his story because he is doing something that impacts not just his life but he is intentionally passing his vision to the generations to come.

We have also heard from others who don't feel as if they can dream anymore. They feel lost in the battle somewhere. During this exercise at one of our conferences, we noticed a couple who sat silently and stared at their workbook without writing a single thought. They told us later in the day that they were stuck and not even sure why. They said the exercise showed them just how empty they felt. The wife said, "It's sad that we don't even know what to dream about for our own family." She began to weep. The good news of this couple's story was, after meeting with us just a few times at our home, they were able to bring out a beautiful vision for not just their family, but their marriage and their lives. What had happened to them was they believed the lie that they were supposed to be stuck in the place of spiritual poverty, lacking blessings, and they would never be fruitful like other families. They felt they just did not deserve it. It's not true, we assured them. Their redemption of their dreams and a vision for their family began with first believing how much the Lord loved them and how He wanted to bless them and their family with abundance.

God did for them what He wants to do for all of us: He gave them courage and a will to start fighting for more for themselves and their family. They are still fighting today to win the battle and climb the mountain of significance. We now love watching them help other families overcome any doubt that they can also live a most adventurous life.

A VISION WITHOUT STATING ITS MEANING OR INTENT AND GIVING ACTION TO IT IS JUST A DREAM.

Read that statement once again. So many die with unfulfilled dreams because they remained just dreams. The transition from your dream to a clearly stated vision with action begins the process of making it a reality for you and your family. There is real power here. Once you and your family believe in the vision and agree on the action to accomplish it, you will see miracles and changed lives, and the best part is that these changes start with those in your household. The ones you love the most.

Let's go back and look at the story of Joshua again. God gave Joshua a big vision. He told him to be strong and courageous, and then the vision transitioned to a plan of action. In order for Joshua to accomplish all that God had shared with him, he needed to get the Israelites moving in a clear, orderly direction. Joshua did not just share the vision of the Promised Land, he put action and direction to it.

> 10 So Joshua ordered the officers of the people:
> 11 "Go through the camp and tell the people, 'Get your provisions ready. Three days from now you will cross the Jordan here to go in and take possession of the land the LORD your God is giving you for your own.'" (Joshua 1:10–11, *AMP*)

Once the vision and direction were clear, the Israelites knew exactly what to do to fulfill the vision. Here is their response:

> 16 Then they answered Joshua, "Whatever you have commanded us we will do, and wherever you send us we will go." (Joshua 1:16, *AMP*)

The Israelites wanted to know that Joshua had a God-given vision and a plan. With these in place they all agreed and started moving toward a common goal. It's the same with your family. This is why your family vision is so powerful. It gives purpose, clear vision, and a way to accomplish it. So please understand this, dads, moms, and grandparents: your family, especially your children, need to know that you are heading in a direction that will bring about abundance and real significance in this adventure. Your kids may not have told you this yet, but believe us, they want it, so now it's time to dream big for your family, your life, your marriage, and your kids. Once the vision is secured, the next step is to pray for the supernatural courage to live it out for your family and all those around you who will be impacted by your very intentional life.

IT'S NEVER TOO LATE

As we mentioned earlier, it's not too late—the purpose for which you were created, the dream and the destiny you were made to fulfill, is still possible. Regardless of your past, your mistakes, your age, and especially how you think others see you, it's all still very possible to discover and live out God's vision for you and your family. Your dream and vision want to come alive, and they are still very much needed. The world needs you to act now to live out God's destiny for you. People are dying every day (physically and spiritually) with the regret of lacking courage; become an example for those for which there is still time. Most important, your family needs you to be strong and courageous and once again seek the most adventurous life. Do not focus on the past; look fully into your present and your future. God is not just a redeemer—He is *your* redeemer.

> [All] are justified and made upright and in right standing with God, freely and gratuitously by His grace (His unmerited favor and mercy), through the redemption which is [provided] in Christ Jesus. (Romans 3:24, *AMP*)

> In Him we have redemption (deliverance and salvation) through His blood, the remission (forgiveness) of our offenses (shortcomings and trespasses), in accordance with the riches and the generosity of His gracious favor. (Ephesians 1:7, *AMP*)

Accept this, believe this, and get ready to live out God's vision for you and your family. Your adventure and destiny start with a vision, the vision God has already given to you or wants to give to you, your spouse, and your children. There is supernatural power here that can change everything: the power in the vision that will make your heart once again fully alive.

IT'S A VISION, NOT A MISSION

Before we jump into how it's done, it's important to understand why we begin with a *vision* statement for your family and not a *mission* statement. A mission statement is really a subset of a greater purpose; the vision *is* the greater purpose God has for you and your family. Missions are something you go and do, something that has a timeline, goals, and measurables, or, in the corporate world, action plans with accountability. The mission, or action, is beneficial to fulfill the vision, but what you first need for your family is the vision—God's vision. Open your heart to desire that God-given revelation about your destiny and where your family needs to go, and then allow the Holy Spirit to show you how to get there, to direct each of your steps.

> In their hearts humans plan their course,but the LORD establishes their steps. (Proverbs 16:9, *AMP*)

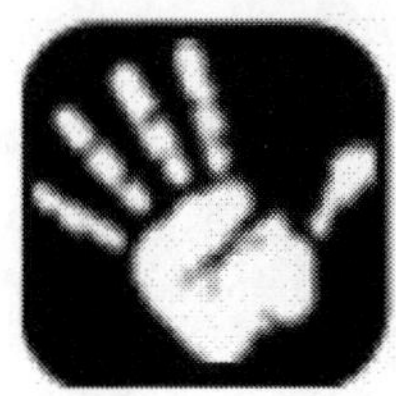

Reflection: Please turn to the accompanying workbook before you move on.

Two

The Purpose of Vision

CAPTURE THE VISION

Creating your vision statement will yield many benefits for you and your family—it will become the vehicle that puts your dream into action. The main benefit, however, is that you will realize through this process that you and your family were meant to live for a greater purpose; God created us to live not in the natural realm but in the supernatural realm. God, the Creator of all things, created your family for a supernatural purpose, and He does not keep that purpose a secret. He wants you to discover it and live in it abundantly. To live this abundant life, we must believe it's truly for us.

supernatural
[Sōōpər'nach(Ə)Rəl]
adjective

1. beyond natural
2. unnaturally or extraordinarily great
3. reflecting God's strength and power

When we don't believe it's for us, we settle for less and become stuck in a life that lacks real supernatural fruit and power. Take a few minutes right now to think about this. Do you feel stuck? Do you feel like others are living more fruitfully? Do others look like they have it all together and, as we say, are blessed? Many believe the abundant life is for others who are more special or gifted, or only for those who have been called into the ministry. Do not be deceived—these gifts are for you and your family.

As much as we know and believe that God is our Creator, we must also know and believe that we have a corruptor. What does he corrupt? The truth. He is a liar. This corruptor does not want you or me to live an abundant life. In fact, satan wants you to live in the opposite of abundance: poverty, lack, scarcity, and insufficiency. He wants you to believe that you will never measure up or that, because of your past, your family, your education, and the choices you have made, God's abundance is not for you. This is a lie. It's important that you know in your heart it's a lie, and you need to call it what it is. God warns us about the enemy's deception in John 8:44 (*AMP*):

> You belong to your father, the devil, and you want to carry out your father's desires. He was a murderer from the beginning, not holding to the truth, for there is no truth in him. When he lies, he speaks his native language, for he is a liar and the father of lies.

We should never live defeated. We are victorious because of the life, death, and resurrection of Jesus. We now have the power and authority to live so. These are not just words, but truth given to us through the Holy Spirit.

> Who is it that is victorious over [that conquers] the world but he who believes that Jesus is the Son of God [who adheres to, trusts in, and relies on that fact]? (1 John 5:5, *AMP*)

In Galatians, Paul tells us that the work of the Holy Spirit's presence in us wants to bring about abundant life for us.

> But the fruit of the [Holy] Spirit [the work which His presence within accomplishes] is love, joy (gladness), peace, patience (an even temper, forbearance), kindness, goodness (benevolence), faithfulness, gentleness (meekness, humility), self-control (self-restraint, continence). Against such things there is no law [that can bring a charge]. (Galatians 5:22–23, AMP)

Appendix A in your workbook contains a brief definition of each of the nine fruits of the Holy Spirit and what it would look like to demonstrate them. Demonstrating the fruit of the Spirit takes action and intentionality, and these things start with clear vision.

Remember that the gifts of the Holy Spirit are beautiful because of the One who gives them. They are not natural gifts (gifts we can manifest with our own strength and power or resources), but supernatural gifts given by God Himself through His Spirit. God sent the Holy Spirit to live in each of us in order to help us live abundantly.

> But the Advocate, the Holy Spirit, whom the Father will send in my name, will teach you all things and will remind you of everything I have said to you. (John 14:26, *AMP*)

This is the Amplified version of the same verse;

> But the Comforter (Counselor, Helper, Intercessor, Advocate, Strengthener, Standby), the Holy Spirit, Whom the Father will send in My name [in My place, to represent Me and act on My behalf], He will teach you all things. And He will cause you to recall (will remind you of, bring to your remembrance) everything I have told you. (John 14:26, *AMP*)

So what has He told us? He has told us that there is fruit in living by the Spirit, and this fruit brings abundance—abundance in love, joy, peace, patience, and so on.

The vision statement is a way for us to move more intentionally into this abundant life when we live according to God's divine purpose for our families. Remember, your adventure and destiny start with a vision, the vision God has already given to you or wants to give to you, your spouse, and your children.

THE VISION BEGINS

In your workbook there is a place for you to draw and color. Yes, we mean color, like you did as a kid. Don't worry about staying in the lines or how artistic you are—just draw and color. Go to the place provided in the workbook now before moving on.

Reflection: Please turn to the accompanying workbook before you move on.

The point of going through this exercise is to see where your family is now and begin to understand that there is so much more that your family can achieve when you dare to dream and get vision. In one of our workshops, one parent asked, "As far as these words that we are writing, are they who we are now or who we want to be?" The answer could be yes to both, but by clearly defining your vision as a family, there is great power. Here's why:

1. A family vision statement becomes your family's true north. If today I said to my family, "Let's get in the car and head north," that could mean a lot of different places. We could end up in Oklahoma City or Kansas City, but if I meant Minneapolis, both Oklahoma City and Kansas City would fall short of the intended destination. In visionary terms, it's imperative to be very specific about where you are going as a family in order to arrive there. The more specific you are with the words you use in your family vision statement, the greater the chance you have of arriving exactly at that place.

2. A family vision statement illustrates the family's contribution and unites the family's commitment. When you involve the entire family in crafting the vision statement, there is an agreement to the contribution as a whole. It is easy to be committed to something individually; who doesn't agree with himself? As each member of the family contributes to the vision, your vision is not only strengthened, it is reinforced by each member who adds value to it. There will be a commitment to a greater purpose or a common adventure that will impact generations and bring about a great reward.

For example, if we agreed as a family that we wanted our home to be a place of ministry by showing hospitality to all who entered our home, we would first have to define what hospitality looked like and what the evidence would be that we were doing it well. We then would have to discuss each of our roles to be sure we were living the vision. This may be as simple as who is expected to keep our house clean, or who will join in to help prepare food and clean up. Each member of the family would have a part in showing hospitality, in making the guests feel welcome. As we live out the vision, we can assess whether we are actually accomplishing what we defined and if there is real evidence or fruit from doing it.

3. A family vision statement instills a team philosophy and communicates the family's uniqueness. The word *team* is big in our family. In fact, it's contained in our family vision statement. A team philosophy brings a family together to work toward a common pursuit, arms locked together to win together. We all have one another's best interests in mind. As with any team, there are individual members, but as your family comes together the unique qualities of each member become family treasures. Uniqueness is part of God's plan. He created each of you uniquely, and your family is meant to benefit from that uniqueness. Do not measure your family to a standard set by any other families. Discuss and celebrate your family's uniqueness. Why are you different? What can you contribute to the Kingdom by that uniqueness?

4. A family vision statement brings about a Godly heritage and will build your family's values, rituals, and traditions. Consider this: do not just leave a legacy; create one. Legacy is part of the transfer process to the next generation. A heritage by definition is something transmitted by or acquired from a predecessor. It is something we will leave our children, intentionally or not. By becoming intentional, we are not leaving that legacy up to chance, and that will change the outcome. Even if you received a good legacy, you can make it better. Once your vision statement is complete, and you start to intentionally do things as a family to make the vision a present reality, you will build on your values and start family rituals. These rituals will become family traditions that will last for generations.

5. A family vision statement becomes your line in the sand. Your family vision statement will be a carefully prepared document that captures your purpose and identifies your values. This document should create emotional energy to motivate and inspire family members toward a common pursuit of excellence. Your vision statement will become the metaphorical line in the sand, beyond which there is no going back to the old way now that you and your family are committed to something so much greater. This line in the sand was another pivotal point of agreement for us. We agreed that there was no turning back from living a life of true significance.

RESULTS OF VISION

When our family began to write our vision statement, we found over time that we were seeing other blessings by being intentional as we lived out our vision. Here are just a few blessings you may also receive; the possibilities are endless.

1. You will find real peace and joy.

> He has made everything beautiful in its time. He also has planted eternity in men's hearts and minds [a divinely implanted sense of a purpose working through the ages which nothing under the sun but God alone can satisfy], yet so that men cannot find out what God has done from the beginning to the end. (Ecclesiastes 3:11, *AMP*)

God gave every one of His creations a divine purpose. God's purpose cannot be accomplished without divine help—only through Him, supernaturally.

Instinctively we know this. We know God created us for something significant; it's the desire of all men and women. Remember the book, *The Top Five Regrets of the Dying*? Everyone wants to know in the end that his or her life had significance.

What if the book had conveyed a different result? What if the people described had done it? What if they had lived a life of significance and adventure? What if they had climbed outside of their comfort zones and did what they were called to do and lived their dream? What if they didn't wait until "someday" or when they had more money or more time because they knew God would provide all they needed, and they did it anyway? That takes real faith and courage. That's how we want to leave this world, with the peace in our hearts that we had enough courage to try and enough faith in knowing God would provide everything we needed to fulfill His divine purpose. There is genuine peace and joy in discovering and living out your divine purpose.

We made the decision to stop everything we were doing and focus exclusively on writing and teaching others about how God redeemed our family through vision and intentionality. Not only were we at peace because we had decided to trust in God's provision, but the more we stepped out in obedience and moved to where God wanted us to be, the more we found it's all we wanted to do; we found great joy in the adventure!

We stepped entirely out of our comfort zone to do what God had put in our hearts, and for the first time in our lives we experienced the fullness of life that God had always intended for us.

Being fully alive in living out your vision doesn't mean you have to leave your job or sell your company. It may mean that you are already at the right place doing the right things, but you need to rethink or repurpose *why* you're doing what you're doing.

We have had the opportunity to help those we refer to as "Kingdom-minded" business owners implement core values or make the core values they have become significant. The power of the process is when their corporate vision and values are in alignment with their family vision and values. Now every decision is intentional because it affects not only the executive team but the owner's family as well. In fact, when implemented well, the corporate vision will have a positive effect on all levels of employees and even many of their families. The business owner is simply a steward of the resources necessary to accomplish a more meaningful success.

Recently we watched two men start a company in the roofing industry. Both were very knowledgeable in sales and roofing products and applications. We had no doubt that they were going to succeed. When we asked them about their vision and business plan, the answer was great.

They explained that the business was going to be a river of blessing that would flow through the company and through their families to accomplish all that the Lord was showing them. They had a vision to impact their employees and company-supported ministries, and this river would flow into their families to help carry out its vision as well.

They believed God owned the company, and He would direct the cash flow in order to carry out a greater purpose for the owners and their families. God gave them the vision, and God would provide the resources. These businessmen had a plan not only for financial success, but something much more significant: Kingdom success.

Visions like this will change the culture through the family and the marketplace. Business owners and individuals can find great supernatural joy and peace when they are in alignment with the vision God wants to carry out through them.

These two men found great joy and peace in carrying out the vision God had given them, and the evidence was clear. So what does this supernatural joy and peace look like? What is the evidence that it exists in our homes and in our children? A supernatural cheerfulness, calm delight (joy), and tranquility of soul where fear no longer rules (peace) will be evidenced by:

- Restored relationships
- Forgiveness
- Sense of thankfulness
- Ability to speak life into others (encouragement)
- Ability to see yourself, and your family, as God sees you
- Desire to serve others
- Generosity

What would happen in our families if we agreed to incorporate the characteristics of joy and peace? Would we not see a supernatural change in our family? What about our children? If our vision statement included words such as joy and peace, and we defined what that looked like (for help on this, see Appendix A), wouldn't completing a vision statement with your family be worth the time and effort?

What about having peace in our homes and with our children? What if supernatural peace rained down on anyone entering your home? Or when they talked to you or your children? The Bible refers to this as peace that surpasses all understanding.

> And God's peace [shall be yours, that tranquil state of a soul assured of its salvation through Christ, and so fearing

> nothing from God and being content with its earthly lot of whatever sort that is, that peace] which transcends all understanding shall garrison and mount guard over your hearts and minds in Christ Jesus. (Philippians 4:7, *AMP*)

When you are living out your destiny within your marriage and family, you are receiving a supernatural joy and peace that surpasses all understanding. This joy and peace will be evident in your lives and to those around you. You will begin living in abundance regardless of what the world says. You can never please the world, but you can please the Creator by living squarely in His purpose. This is so exciting. What an adventure!

2. You will know that you are pleasing to your Creator. You will receive supernatural joy and peace because you are pleasing to your Creator. If you have children, don't you receive great joy when you watch your kids chase after the gifts and talents God gave them? It's pleasing to us as parents. Likewise, it's pleasing to our heavenly Father when we pursue the gifts He's put into our hands. Among these gifts are a dream to fulfill your destiny and the vision to accomplish it.

People miss out on living this destiny and vision when they pursue worldly things. Scripture warns us of this in the Apostle Paul's letter to the Colossians.

> And set your minds and keep them set on what is above (the higher things), not on the things that are on the

> earth. For [as far as this world is concerned] you have died, and your [new, real] life is hidden with Christ in God. When Christ, Who is our life, appears, then you also will appear with Him in [the splendor of His] glory. (Colossians 3:2–4, *AMP*)

If we believe that Christ is our life, then shouldn't we pursue what He has for us and forget the things of the world because it is pleasing to Him? Do we believe that He is greater than the world? That He can supply all of our needs? Do we believe that He is willing to give us the desires of our hearts in pursuit of our destiny because it is pleasing to Him?

Reread the last paragraph. Do you really believe that? If you do, then the power of this vision will help catapult you into what He has for you. Not just for you, but for your marriage and your family. God's character is to give, and give abundantly. As you take each step in living out your vision and moving into your destiny, you will be richly blessed (happy, to be envied, and spiritually prosperous—with life-joy and satisfaction in God's favor and salvation, regardless of their outward conditions).

For our family, we witnessed four generations changed because of our obedience. We watched our children become confident in who they are and accept who God made them. We have seen many other families change because we had the courage to take the steps outlined in this book for you. Why? Because you are pleasing to the One Who created you.

3. You will be an example to your children and grandchildren. One afternoon our daughter-in-law Halli relayed a story about our daughter, Cori, encouraging someone at her church youth group. A girl in the group told the other kids about her family and how her father had lost his job. It had really shaken the family because they weren't sure what was going to happen.

After listening to this girl's story, Cori asked if she could speak to the group about what she had just heard. Once given the nod, Cori told the girl that her dad had gone through something similar. She spoke about how she watched me try to find my way by discovering ways to be useful, successful, and even significant. She said she observed me for months as I worked through many different ideas, and for the most part none of them had succeeded.

Cori then said one day her mom and dad called the family together and told them we were going to dramatically change our family's lifestyle to chase what we believed God was calling us to do. She said we, as parents, had felt called to help equip other parents, and we were going to leave everything we had known as success and pursue this calling.

She told the girl that she watched us begin to live out a courageous life of helping other families. She said it helped her to see what really mattered because she wanted to do the same: live out her destiny. She explained that sometimes God uses these life events to shake us and move us closer to where we are supposed to be, and that her dad may just be on the verge of doing something significant. "Don't worry; tell your dad that you believe in him and God is getting ready to do something great in him. Become his encourager," Cori told the girl.

When we heard this story we were taken aback by how our fifteen-year-old daughter had seen not just our story play out, but how our willingness to pursue God's calling for our lives had impacted her life. She also realized that, even though we'd had to change our lifestyle (I do not mean that living out your vision leads to a life of poverty—that's a lie), it was well worth the blessing our family received, and is receiving, in the process. We as parents had impacted Cori by living out the vision God planted in us with intentionality.

Soon after, Cori reminded us that our vision statement, hanging on the wall in our living room, read, "Our family wants to make a difference in the lives of other families." We were doing it! We were living the vision and the destiny we believed God had given our family. When we composed our vision statement, we included our kids in the process, and "making a difference by helping other families" was something we had all agreed on. Cori had intentionally made a difference in another family by encouraging this young girl.

I have come to understand one of the reasons we are losing some of our kids to the world is because they have not seen real manifested fruit in their own homes. This vision statement and the power that comes from creating it is a way to show our children and the world real manifested fruit. After your vision statement is complete, remain intentional in living the life it represents.

4. You become hope for other families. Regardless of your marital status, you have the power to impact others and live a significant life. Single moms need other single moms to assure them that they can also have a family of vision and significance. It's the same with single dads and other forms of family. Regardless of your family's form, your children need you to show them how to live a courageous, intentional life with vision.

We have had pastors of different denominations confide to us that the families inside their church look no different than the families outside. Could it be from a lack of vision to live out a courageous, intentional life? We don't want to simplify the problem with a one-sentence solution, but there is great power in vision and the process of getting all forms of family into agreement over one. For example, if you drew a picture of a spiritually successful family, every form of family would say, "We want that for our family." Once the vision is created and action is put toward living out the vision, great change happens. The fruit of the vision can only add adventure, excitement, and fulfillment to a marriage and a family like nothing else when the vision is poured out from the Holy Spirit.

The best news is that by living out this great adventure of your vision and the courageous, intentional life it brings, you will impact everyone around you by your example and the fruit that comes from it. We have had so many families tell us they have watched our family and want whatever it is we have. They've seen us go from living the pointless, empty American Dream to a life of Holy Spirit abundance.

What if one family in each neighborhood made a decision to receive a vision from God and live it out with intentionality? What would happen if that family helped other families through the same process? Would it not change our neighborhoods, our churches, and our cities because of the fruit being multiplied in other homes?

We believe most families want more, more for their marriages, more for their children, and more for the others they care about. What if you set the example? What if you took the steps and lived out the God-given vision for your life? You and your family could change the world. Believe it.

Here are a few questions. Would you do it for your children and grandchildren? Will you commit right now to the process outlined in this book and get into agreement with your spouse to finish it? The next generation was our motivation to become intentional. As we said, we saw the world having a greater impact on our children than we were. This process was a game changer for us, and it can be for your family as well.

5. Your marriage will have greater purpose. In our conferences, Danielle and I do something kind of cheesy. We demonstrate what a picture of a marriage should look like for our children. The point of the illustration is that our kids need to see this picture so our sons know what type of wife to pursue and our daughters know what kind of man to marry. If our kids don't know what this looks like, then the world will define it for them. This is something Danielle and I did not want to leave to chance. So, here goes! You have to use your imagination, but we know you will see it.

We describe the picture starting with me sitting on a horse. The horse is the power that will take us on this life's adventure. I tell the audience that I have the power to accomplish great things, and this power comes from the Holy Spirit. The color of the horse is not really important, but our horse is white because I know Danielle, as a young girl, dreamed of being rescued by a knight on a white horse. Not that she needed to be rescued because she already had a Savior, but what she wanted was to go on an adventure with someone who would lead and protect her. Don't all little girls play with dolls and horses and have dreams similar to this? I know mine did. What they really want is to live a life of courageous intentionality. Sure, they want to raise a family and be cherished, but they also desire to be led into adventure.

Back to the illustration: I'm on a white horse, and I'm holding a sword. The sword is doubled-edged to fight for the things of God and against the enemy. My bride wants to know I'm willing to fight for her, our family, and the vision that led us to live a courageous life. On the back of the horse sits my wife, Danielle, with one arm around my waist. In her other hand she grips a sword as well. She is equipped to fight, mostly against the things I can't see.

I then look directly at the men in the room and say, "Understand this, men—I can't see the back of my head." No matter how I try, I can't, not even with a mirror, so my wife's job on this adventure is to help me notice the things I'm missing while we lead our family forward on the adventure. She uses her sword for the same purposes: to fight for what is of God and to slay and rebuke the things that are not.

I've learned something wonderful about my wife that I wish I'd learned long ago: she hears from the Holy Spirit differently than I do, and she's more open to His leading. Men, don't take offense here, but your wife is different because she was created differently. In fact, there are only two places in the Bible where God speaks of giving us a helper. One was a wife, in Genesis 2:18, and the other was when Jesus was about to ascend into heaven.

> However, I am telling you nothing but the truth when I say it is profitable (good, expedient, advantageous) for you that I go away. Because if I do not go away, the Comforter (Counselor, Helper, Advocate, Intercessor, Strengthener, Standby) will not come to you [into close fellowship with you]; but if I go away, I will send Him to you [to be in close fellowship with you]. (John 16:7, *AMP*)

I often stop, look at my wife, and ask her questions. I know we are already in agreement over the vision, but I check to see if we are going in the right direction and if I am missing anything. These questions may sound like this:

> Babe, what are you hearing?
> What do you see?
> What's the Spirit telling you?

Why do I ask these questions? Because, as I mentioned earlier, I can't see the back of my head. What does the Holy Spirit do? Lead us into all truth. Danielle is what I now refer to as my Holy Spirit on the ground. In other words, I am so thankful for her ability to hear and willingness to be led because of how she was made for me in the covenant of our marriage.

So on this horse we lead our family into this vision we have all agreed upon, and our children get to watch as their dad and mom live a most courageous, intentional life ~ in their proper roles. How exciting and fun is that?

We can tell you, of all the things we have ever done, mostly in our own power, strength, and resources, we have never had as much fun as we are having at this very moment. We love it, and we know our children love it as well. They are excited by the example we have been to them, and we are confident your children will be excited by the example you will set for them as well.

Now, this example is no less important for other forms of family. Even if you are a single parent or in any other form of family, your children need to see the example of marriage the way God intended. We have not always been the best example, but we understand the importance, now more than ever. So, regardless of the form of your family right now, be intentional about teaching your children God's intent for marriage and family. God's way is the best way to experience His supernatural power.

In addition to what we have listed above, there is another benefit of getting clear vision for your family. One family we coached seemed to always be in so much stress. They talked about how their home seemed to be in conflict and the kids acted out in dramatic ways such as yelling, slamming doors, crying, and even once the daughter shouted at her mom, "I hate our family!" We all began to pray for God to help this family to see how they were being attacked so they could battle and fight for peace. As it turned out, the family vision statement gave them the answer.

As this family took courage and completed the vision statement, they came to their own conclusion that their house was so stressful because they said yes to everything and everyone. Because they had no true north, they were involved in way too much and tried to please everyone without even knowing why.

What they told us a few months later was that their vision statement not only united their family in a clear direction, it gave them the ability to say no to many things that didn't matter because they did not line up with where they were going. "So," they said, "we now have the ability and peace to be intentional even when we say no to certain things." Now their family had more time, more peace, and less chaos. They said the process was freeing for their whole family and gave them clarity of vision.

STEP OUT AND BEGIN

As you begin the process of composing your God-given vision statement for your family, you will begin to see the evidence of fruit right away as you and your spouse get into agreement and get the kids involved in the process.

For you, as parents, this process may lead you out of your comfort zone just a bit. That's okay. Do not let your past failures determine your success in this undertaking. Even if you have children old enough to know your past or who do not believe you will follow through with this effort, do not turn back. We've talked with parents whose children doubted their commitment to finish the process. These parents either allowed their children to determine the outcome, or they overcame by finishing well. You can overcome. Don't let the enemy whisper lies to you. Do not let your children witness another unfinished attempt. You have the power to succeed, take authority over your home, and lead your family. God gave you that power, and He will accompany you through to completion (see Philippians 1:6).

Many of the parents we have helped equip are now living a supernatural life, and everyone has been changed. One family told us their kids remind them that they love their "new" dad and mom. Remember, your kids need to see you succeed, and they want to live in abundance with you. The supernatural life is more fun and fulfilling than anything you have ever done, ever! Step out of your comfort zone. This is where God will show up.

We want to encourage you to take the time to draw your family picture and think through what your family looks like and means to you. For some this may be a time of reflection that brings back memories and even pain. Some families are really messy, and that's okay. God can do great things when a light is put on what has been kept in the dark.

At one of our workshops we had two generations of the same family present, and from this exercise we realized the proverbial elephant was in the room. As they drew and then began to describe their family to the group, the pictures from the two generations were almost identical, except the youngest son had included a sister in his picture. It took courage for this sibling to include his estranged sister in his picture. We realized later that he included her because he wanted to talk about how to restore her to the family. He told us in a subsequent meeting that he never understood why no one wanted to talk about her, and he believed that God would restore his whole family.

In another one of our workshops we listened to a single mom describe her family using a picture with her ex-husband included. As she talked about her family, she told the group that even though they were divorced, her ex-husband was still a part of the family and would be influencing the girls they had together. She said it was hard for her to not include the father of her girls in the picture. She did preface her description by telling the group that in the small detail of the picture she gave him horns on top of his head.

The picture of your family will change through this process, but it is important to draw what it looks like right now to begin the transformation to what God is already doing.

Complete the picture in your workbook, if you have not already done so and answer the remaining questions for this chapter.

Reflection: Please turn to the accompanying workbook before you move on.

Three

Test Your Vision

MAKE THE DISTINCTION

Let's distinguish clearly the difference between a dream and a vision before we go any further. A vision is something we see while we're awake. It is an image or impression of something now or in the future. A vision is seen in our heads and felt in our hearts. We can almost see it clearly enough to take a picture of it. A dream is something you have while you're asleep. Both can be vivid and very real. Both can have great meaning. The reason we want to distinguish between them is because your vision for your family will come as a result of seeing (while you're awake) what your family could look like or what you could be doing now and in the future. If you had a dream that had real meaning, you could envision it after you awoke and ponder it in your heart to determine what it meant and what you should do, if anything. Although a vision can be something you receive in a supernatural way, it will take intentional steps to put the vision into words that will cause you and your family to take action to bring it to fulfillment. The steps put forth in these pages, taken apart from the Holy Spirit's guidance, will bring some fruit and success for your family; however, if you take the time to open your spiritual eyes and ears and allow the Lord to help you through the process, the results will be supernatural.

Many people talk about dreams and visions as being interchangeable, but we are only going to talk about the intentional steps of creating and recording the vision that will come from your head and your heart as the Holy Spirit leads. Remember - A vision with action and intentionality will change the outcome for your family.

Over the past few years we've helped many families compose their vision statements, and during the process we've found that families who have not completed a vision statement usually fall into one of two camps: those who have received a vision (they have thought about it, and it was good) but don't follow through with it, and those who believe they've never received or thought about a vision at all and want one. Let's examine both so you can move forward in the power you will receive in your family vision.

CAMP COMFORT ZONE

The first camp believes God has given them a vision, meaning they have a passion for something they know is from God, and they may even have some direction to implement their vision. They can talk about their vision in great detail with excitement, but something happened along the way that derailed it. They either can't find the time, or they're just too fearful to step out. For many, not moving toward their vision is a consequence of becoming comfortable in their lifestyles. This is a stumbling block we call the "comfort zone."

What is the "comfort zone," and how do families get there? It's a virtual camp where the parents—the campers—find themselves in the precarious position of trying to balance finances, schedules, work, and even the family vacations. It's a place of busyness where you still may hear from God, but the daily to-do lists keep you from following through on what you hear. You may not even realize you're stuck in the comfort zone because life seems to be working out just fine, or at least you may think so. The comfort zone is not necessarily a bad place. In fact, God can use the comfort zone as a place of preparation. It allows families to learn how to function well. The stumbling block is when the comfort zone becomes monotonous and there's no sense of significant accomplishment or spiritual growth. When a family becomes stagnant, the enemy can move in and begin to have a greater influence. This can become a real problem for everyone in the household.

When we first got married we had excitement and anticipation of doing great things as a family. We spent hours talking about our vision. We, like most newly married couples, knew we could make a difference and set out to make the vision real. It's clear to us now that something began to happen that took us off course for our great adventure.

What took us off course was getting too comfortable with our success in the material world for the sake of proving that we had arrived or made it. It was more about showing off how well we were doing, and eventually this lifestyle became about parties and traveling to entertain ourselves. We lost our greater purpose in our comfort and lifestyle and felt like we could play with matches and not get burned. It was truly a life of selfishness, which brought no glory to God.

We played with matches all right, but eventually we found ourselves surrounded by a full-fledged forest fire, fueled by our own desires. We finally realized that the world was having a bigger impact on us than we were having on it. In other words, our light was no longer the light of Christ but a flashy neon sign that read, "Let us eat and drink, for tomorrow we will be dead" (1 Cor. 15: 32, *AMP*)

We had fallen into a pit of worldliness, and our children—all five of them—eventually became casualties in the war we were losing. After several years we turned back to the Lord for help. We experienced many setbacks, but we refused to be defeated, and slowly we regained the strength through the Holy Spirit to not only recapture the ground we had surrendered but also gain an even bigger victory as we allowed God to move our vision to a deeper level. Much of the material for our family conferences and online learning comes from the struggle and eventual victories we experienced.

Our vision didn't change; it just grew in depth and potential. Whereas our original focus centered on our newly formed family, our communication, and beginning a Christian way of life, our new focus expanded to other families as well. During our family discussion it became a consensus that we all wanted to make a difference in the lives of families. As our family listened to the Spirit and crafted our vision statement, little did we know to what extent we would soon be equipping other families. When we realized our vision included helping other families, we knew this vision was not only for us as parents but for us all.

As it turns out, they've all played a role in bringing about our calling, from video and production to blogs and helping out at our conferences. They've played a big part in the family gatherings we organize once a month in our home, sharing life with other kids and young adults as we all pour into (encourage) families and they pour into us. In other words, they've seen the vision come fully alive. They've seen the fruit of our obedience, and in turn they've seen how God is using them. We know because of their own fruit that they've all been greatly impacted—we've seen God move each of them into His purpose for their lives.

STEPPING OUT OF THE COMFORT ZONE

God's vision is the motivation to move forward. Revisiting or remembering this will result in ordinary families doing extraordinary things. Can you imagine what the world would be like without families such as the von Trapps or the ten Booms? The von Trapps are remembered for their courage in resisting a regime. You most likely remember them from *The Sound of Music*. The Ten Booms were a heroic family who saved hundreds of Jews during the Holocaust. You may remember their story from *The Hiding Place*.

More recently we've witnessed the power of the Graham family, who now have a multigenerational legacy of bringing people to

Christ through global crusades. Or the Green family, who left their comfort zone to resist a government mandate that challenged the beliefs under which they built the Hobby Lobby chain of stores.

These were ordinary families living comfortable, ordinary lives who chose, as a family, to live out a larger vision. The world is a better place as a result of their lives of purpose. You must get uncomfortable for a purpose.

One of the many "uncomfortable" things our family enjoys doing is storm chasing. We chase storms, mostly hurricanes and tornadoes, with a team. The team with whom we chase storms believes it's important to help rescue others who don't even know they need to be rescued, both physically and spiritually. We accomplish this by being at the wrong place at the right time, warning communities about impending storms and initiating search and rescue efforts when homes or communities are affected. Afterward we engage in disaster relief by ministering to families in several ways: feeding them, cleaning up with them, and rebuilding alongside them.

Recently, two of my sons and I were following a National Weather Service severe storm warning when we found ourselves on the wrong side of a storm that had taken an unexpected turn. While we were repositioning to get back to the safe side, we experienced large hail, slippery, muddy roads, and torrential rains. Once out of danger I noticed my fingers were still white-knuckled as I gripped the steering wheel, and my heart was pounding out of my chest. I asked myself, "Why do we do this?" For the last twenty minutes, as I'd prayed for our team's safety and tried to keep the car out of a ditch, I hadn't been completely enjoying myself. The adventure had taken the boys and me out of our comfort zones.

As we recovered and continued to follow this particular storm, we witnessed a magnificent tornado on the plains of New Mexico, where no one could get hurt. As the tornado tore across the open space, we watched a small creek grow into a rushing river on both sides of the road where our car had just been. Then we saw a beautiful, full rainbow. That's when it hit me: we were called to do this.

Chasing tornadoes and helping others in their aftermath aren't things our family just went out and started doing a few days ago. We've been studying and tracking storms for many years, and we know that this is not for everyone, but it is for us. We've saved lives by warning communities of approaching storms through the National Weather Service, local media, or just driving along small town streets with our windows down, honking the horn and yelling, "Take cover! There's a tornado heading this way!" Indeed, we were made for this.

It's at the moment of danger and warning that we become fully alive in our purpose. Then, as the danger passes, we lift families out of the rubble and help them begin to rebuild their lives. It's not comfortable to witness heartbroken men, women, and children who have just lost everything they held dear. It's not comfortable to drive for hours, eat junk food, and return in the wee hours of the morning, but God has called us to step out, and we know it.

When my middle son, Noah, was ten years old, he was faced with an uncomfortable situation. While serving water, ice, and sandwiches to lines of families in cars after Hurricane Rita had devastated Orange County, Texas, the police told us to stop because we were impeding traffic flow and endangering ourselves by running through the street. They were serious and even threatened to arrest us if we continued. While many of the men stopped to figure out another way to serve the families affected by the hurricane, Noah continued to run from car to car taking sandwich orders. He'd then head back to the tent to make the sandwiches and gather ice, and then dash back to each car to deliver it. When we confronted him, he said, "Dad, they're hungry; I can't stop." The rest of us decided that if they were going to haul us to jail, we were going to feed as many people as we could first. Because of Noah, a typically law-abiding young man, we all resolved to get uncomfortable for the benefit of others. Noah had a clear vision and comfortable or not, he was determined to achieve it.

We want to live our lives with hearts that are fully alive, out of our natural or worldly comfort zone. We want the same for our family—and yours.

As we have said, the turning point for us was to recapture the vision, write it down and bring intentionality to it. Because we got the whole family involved in the creation of the vision statement, we had some level of family accountability to keep us on track. Camp Comfort Zone can be avoided, but if you are here it's not too late to bring your vision back alive.

THE STUFF CAMP

The second camp of families who've never composed a vision statement are those who don't feel as if they've heard from God in any way about the vision or destiny for their lives. They say they want one, but they haven't received it, or if they did, they somehow missed it.

After listening to families who have fallen into this camp, we first begin to help them by understanding where they are in pursuing Jesus and the Holy Spirit. In most cases, we discover they're not hearing because they're not asking and pursuing. It's like asking for the gifts of the Holy Spirit (Galatians 5:22) without having a relationship with the One Who gives the gifts. If this is you, you must first want more to receive more. For example, if we want to receive more in our marriage, we have to want it first. We must deeply desire it and be praying and listening in order to receive it. We can't tell you how many times in the last few years we have said to each other that we want more—for our family, our marriage, and our relationship with Jesus, who gave us His Spirit—then prayed specifically for what we desired. Do you want more? Say it now: "I want more." Write this statement on your bathroom mirror so you'll see it when you first wake up. This will remind you to speak these words of life daily, if not continually.

> "'In the last days, God says, I will pour out my Spirit on all people. Your sons **and** daughters will prophesy, your young men will see **visions**; your old men will dream **dreams**.'" (Acts 2:17 AMP) emphasis added

God is a giver of visions, and He speaks to everyone, especially families, because He created them for a grand purpose, which we'll discuss in later chapters. For now, believe that God has a vision for you and your family, and ask the Holy Spirit to reveal it to you. In our case, we'd muffled the Holy Spirit's voice with all the stuff under which we'd buried our lives, but with time and intentionality we regained the ability to hear and listen to God. You can, too.

We have a friend who tells us almost every time we get together what God has said to him. The passion and depth of what he sees in his vision are quite extraordinary. We can't tell you how many times we've told him to write all these things down. "Start now!" we tell him. "Don't let these ideas and pictures in your head leave you." We've given him outlines to help him begin. We've poured out encouragement, and we've sent him emails and links to blogs relating to subjects about which he is passionate, but nothing has come of it yet.

What's happened to him is something we fight against every day. It's the stuff—stuff that should be done, needs to be done, or really makes no difference if it gets done or not. Most of the stuff is a distraction from what our Creator wants us to be doing, so we encourage you to make a list of the stuff and rank it by importance. We have provided space in the workbook for this exercise and you will be prompted at the end of the chapter if you do not take the time to make the list now. For each distraction, ask yourself a question: does this move me closer to or farther away from what God has called me to do? Is it a distraction, or does it make my heart come fully alive? It is imperative to deal with the stuff appropriately and move forward. Remember, the enemy wants you distracted and living in chaos without clear vision. Wherever you are is okay, but it's not okay to stay there. Be intentional.

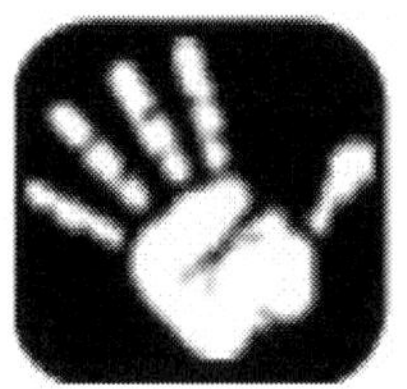

Reflection: Please turn to the accompanying workbook before you move on.

If you believe God has given you a vision toward a destiny, you should test it with the Holy Spirit to make sure it's not just a distraction from something else you should be doing. Distractions are everywhere and come at us by the truckload every day to keep us from living out our vision.

TEST YOUR VISION

Pray for the distractions to fade into the background as you focus on what the Lord is speaking to you about vision. Be of great courage and ask Him to make it abundantly clear. As words come into your mind, write them down in the space provided in the workbook. You may be surprised at how many words you receive and how quickly.

How do you test your vision with the Holy Spirit? Ask yourself: does your vision bring you excitement, joy, peace? Do you think about it often as the Spirit brings it back to your mind? Do you find yourself telling others about it? Can you see yourself and your family accomplishing it in visions and even dreams? Does it make you nervous but at the same time excited? These are all indications that the Holy Spirit is leading you.

The opposite would be true if the vision was not from the Holy Spirit. You would not be excited, it would not come into your mind often unless you forced it, you would be scared (different from nervous), and it would not make you fully alive. You would find no comfort there. Most of all, you would not feel like shouting it out from the rooftops or every time there is a break in the conversations with family, friends, and coworkers.

If you answered yes to most or all of the questions above, you're probably much farther along than you think to having a God-given vision. At this point it's important to stop reading and write down the top five to ten bullet points of what you believe this vision means for your family and others. There is space provided for this exercise in the workbook. Let the words flow; if they come to mind, write them down. Words will turn into phrases, and phrases will turn into complete thoughts. Please complete the workbook before proceeding. Allow time for the words, thoughts, and concepts to flow; this is a very important step in the process. If you are staring at the blank space in the workbook, don't fret; that is okay. Pray and wait—the words will come.

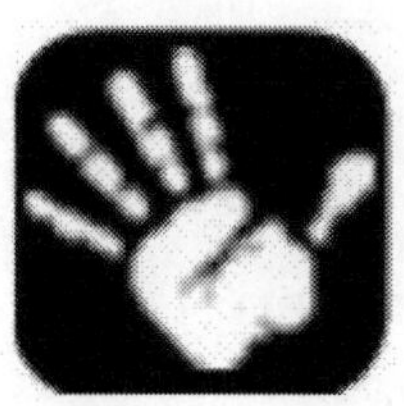

Reflection: Please turn to the accompanying workbook before you move on.

Now that you've written down what you believe your vision means for you and others, take some time to dwell on what you've jotted down, and ask the Holy Spirit to give you more. Talk to your spouse or someone who knows you well about what you wrote and what the Spirit is adding to it. Then you'll be able to incorporate these points into this process. You'll love the outcome.

You may be saying to yourself, "No way, this vision can't be from God. He can't be talking to me. He must mean someone else." If you don't know the stories about how God chose others who said the same thing, I suggest you read some great Kingdom stories about Moses, Joshua, and Abraham. These are timeless accounts of men doing stuff who got a call from the Lord to move into something greater than they could have ever done in the natural realm. These accounts are truly supernatural.

Moses even said, "No, Lord, you got the wrong guy. I'm not equipped to do this; in fact, I'm the least likely one to go (paraphrased)." This is what's so great about your story: you can't do it on your own. The Lord will lead you supernaturally as you trust in Him each day.

If you think you don't have a vision or maybe you missed it, you're still in a great place. First, believe that God created you for a purpose. He will communicate this purpose to you in many ways but mostly through a process that begins with writing your family vision statement. We received most of our direction for our family, our business, and eventually our ministry through the process of composing our vision statement and revisiting it regularly with our family for deeper revelation. We believe the destiny to help other families was revealed through this process, which will empower you and your family for His purposes as well.

In the chart provided in the workbook, write down what you see as the God-given gifts and talents you feel you've received. Write down what you enjoy doing. What has He already begun in you? If you're married, have your spouse do the same. We'll come back and incorporate this later, but it's important that you do it now.

No matter what camp you fall into, you must begin. You must do something to move forward. Have faith or pray for the courage to walk into more faith, but begin. Remember, there are so many people waiting for you to live this adventurous life, especially your family. You are beginning to create your family's legacy. Be intentional—it matters.

Reflection: Please turn to the accompanying workbook before you move on.

Four

Coming Into Agreement for Vision

PRAYING FOR VISION

Are you ready to begin building the foundation for your family vision statement? This chapter will give you the tools and intentional steps necessary to develop a tangible family vision statement and prepare you to involve your children in the adventure.

The purpose of Chapters 4 and 5 is to give you a step-by-step process for developing your vision with intentionality for your family. By the time you get to Chapter 6 you should have at least completed a written framework for your family vision statement. If you are going through this process as a group or with another family, it would be good for you to help keep each other accountable with a time line to complete each step and chapter. In Chapter 6 we will include a finished picture of our family vision statement for you to see if you get stuck. So get your pens ready to start taking intentional notes and make some significant progress through the workbook: let's begin.

First, take a few minutes right now to ask God for His involvement. He wants to be a part of this process with your family. He wants to be invited into this process with you and your spouse. He created your family for a purpose and as you allow Him to come alongside you He will help you discover or rediscover your vision. God will use all your experiences, good and bad, to bring you into His purpose. Do not be discouraged; whatever the form of your family is at this point, it will always be better if you invite Him into the process. Turn to the workbook to journal your thoughts and consider some thought-provoking questions. Although this chapter's primary purpose is to come into agreement as a couple, do not skip this part if you are a single parent. You can use these exercises to ensure you're in agreement with the Father. If you are married, you will find plenty of benefits to getting into agreement on your family vision. Complete the exercises as a couple. The benefits gained here will become helpful in many circumstances, so do not rush through or become impatient if this short chapter takes you several attempts to accomplish. Many times when Danielle and I came to a standstill, we had to walk away and come back together later. You must commit to coming back to it until you find common ground.

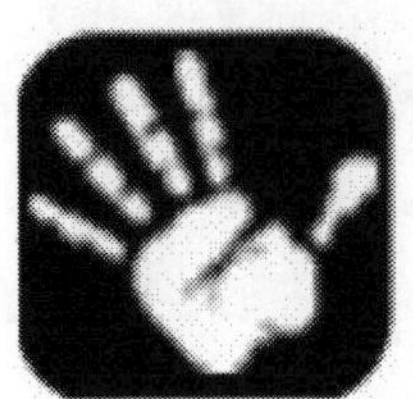

Reflection: Please turn to the accompanying workbook before you move on.

The next intentional step will help you and your spouse get into agreement over words. Why? Because words matter. The very words that will comprise your vision statement will be foundational in the sense that all other action or practical steps will be built upon these words. You will also see how the words your children use when you get them involved in the process will be significant to them as you display your vision for your family and others to see. The words you choose will also hold spiritual significance to you that will stand the test of time for your family. Using words that describe who your family is now and, more importantly how you see your family in the future will give your family a clearer vision of what your family is spiritually evolving to as time goes by.

Remember, these words may be your foundation but are not a beginning in themselves because Jesus laid the foundations of His truth upon which everything else, even your vision will be built. Read in 1 Corinthians 3:10-15 (NASB) to affirm the importance of this step:

> **10** According to the grace of God which was given to
> me, like a wise master builder I laid a foundation, and
> another is building on it. But each man must be careful
> how he builds on it.
> **11** For no man can lay a foundation other than the one
> which is laid, which is Jesus Christ.
> **12** Now if any man builds on the foundation with gold,
> silver, [d]precious stones, wood, hay, straw,

> **13** each man's work will become evident; for the day will show it because it is *to be* revealed with fire, and the fire itself will test [e]the quality of each man's work.
> **14** If any man's work which he has built on it remains, he will receive a reward.
> **15** If any man's work is burned up, he will suffer loss; but he himself will be saved, yet so as through fire.

Because your words matter and have a spiritual significance that add to what Jesus has already done, you also will receive blessing because of your willingness to be intentional in this process.

Use the chart in the workbook to write down at least ten of the descriptive words that spoke most deeply and powerfully to your heart as you considered your family living out each word God brought to your mind. These words will bless your family as they become the foundation of your vision for them.

If you need help choosing words or maybe a few ideas to get you started, flip to Appendix B in the back of this book. There you'll find values words and fruit of the Spirit words, which we've defined to help you decide what to use in your family vision statement. What is your heart saying about who you are as a family? What is God telling you?

Here's another way to think about this process and its meaning for your family: if someone else was to describe your family in a meaningful way, what words would you want them to use to define you, your spouse, and your children? As you choose these words, your heart should come alive because they will not only describe you but bless you as well.

If you're married, share this exercise with your spouse and get into agreement. Pray that you easily get into agreement over these words for your family. If you're not married, pray to be in agreement with the Lord regarding your family's vision. Pray for peace and excitement about your vision statement. It should be compelling. Whatever your circumstances are right now, pray. Let the Holy Spirit direct your steps. Pray for revelation about your vision and the words that will be connected to it. Again, there is power in these words. Pray for these words to flash before your eyes like flying neon signs, then write them down in the space provided so they will be available to revisit as you continue the process of developing your family vision statement. For those who love lists, we placed the Agreement column provided in the workbook to check off when you have come into agreement.

The significance and importance of this seemingly simple activity cannot be overemphasized. This very exercise becomes your line in the sand. You are gaining victory, possibly reconquering surrendered ground, with every powerful word regarding your family that you accept from the Lord. Please do not take this part of the process lightly. The words you have just written may very well be the centerpiece that will transform your family supernaturally into God's destiny.

After completing this exercise, ponder what you have just accomplished and thank the Lord for what He is doing in you and your family. The blessing that began here will reverberate for generations.

Visit www.c2family.com/videos and watch the *Words Matter* video for more coaching.

Reflection: Please turn to the accompanying workbook before you move on.

GETTING INTO AGREEMENT

God created you and your spouse for the same destiny. Perhaps the biggest and most important step in this process is for you and your spouse to get into agreement.

Getting into agreement is not always easy. It can take time to work through this part of the process, and that's okay. Many couples have shared with us about what they learned as they tried to get into agreement with each other. You may discover you don't communicate very well, and you may feel something is getting in the way of moving forward. One couple said that they realized they didn't even like each other very much anymore, and the whole conversation had been very difficult.

If this is the case, we recommend setting the vision statement aside for a time and working on your communication or other issues that need to be addressed before continuing. Visit the Resources section at the back of the book for more guidance on communication and healthy marriages.

When we first started to work through this process for our family, we knew we had to be very intentional for this to become a reality. We both had to ask for forgiveness in the areas where we were weak, and we also asked for strength and patience as God worked through both of us. Once we felt we'd received grace and mercy from each other, God showed up and instilled excitement and revelation in us both. Remember Jesus's words:

> "If a house is divided against itself, that house cannot stand."
> (Mark 3:25, *AMP*)

Fight against the enemy together with prayer and agreement. We know that the enemy wants to divide you. If you allow this exercise to divide you, the enemy has won because satan knows full well the power that exists here for your family. That's why this vision statement process is extremely important; it will unify and strengthen your family. This is certainly not what the enemy wants, so even though it may be difficult, press on. Start by agreeing on one thing, even if it's small. For instance, start by getting into agreement that you will not let the enemy win over your family. Keep talking until you're able to work through it.

Remember this always: the Lord will never call you into one destiny and your spouse into another that would ultimately divide your marriage. This is a form of disunion from the enemy. There was a reason for your marriage covenant, and it should not be divided or torn apart.

> So they are no longer two, but one flesh. What therefore God has joined together, let not man put asunder (separate). (Matthew 19:6, *AMP*)

> That is why a man leaves his father and mother and is united to his wife, and they become one flesh. (Genesis 2:24, *AMP*)

We also want to be clear that moving into your marriage destiny together does not mean that you are doing everything together. We have seen couples who have two very different and successful careers, but when we speak to them about family and destiny they are both undeniably on the same page. They both get excited talking about their children and raising them with intentionality. The couple works in unison for their family because they are in agreement on the family's vision and legacy. They have also agreed on why they both work and how this plays into the overall plan. This is their vision. It's exciting to hear them share.

Make sure as you talk about your family vision, your marriage, and your destiny that it brings you together with excitement and joy as you set out to live it. If it divides your relationship, know that this is not from God. You might need to spend more time on communication and getting into agreement on a vision that unites rather than divides.

The other important thing to remember is that your kids desperately need you to work it out and be the example for them. If you're divorced, single, or a blended family, make no mistake—you are still a family. Do not be discouraged about your current situation; God is your Redeemer and wants you to live abundantly. You are where you are, but don't stay there. God never rules any family out for destiny, and He's already moving ahead of you, bringing about the best possible outcome for your family. Move forward and receive His blessings.

As we started to work through this process of agreement, we first agreed to talk until we reached a consensus. This sometimes took multiple attempts to get to where we both agreed, but as time went on it became easier. Stick to this process, or, as we say in our family, C2 it!

Kids are very smart, and if you try to move forward in bringing them into the process before you and your spouse are in total agreement, they'll sniff it out. This process is intended to unify your family so you can begin your great adventure. Take the time to get into agreement over these words. Write them down. Be intentional.

Visit www.c2family.com/videos and watch the *Getting into Agreement* video for more coaching.

THE BEGINNINGS OF YOUR FAMILY VISION STATEMENT

At this point you should have two tasks completed. First, you have written down any ideas or thoughts you believe God is telling you about your vision through the gifts, talents, or even dreams you recognize as coming from the Lord. This exercise helped move you closer to what the Lord is already telling or showing you. Second, you have begun your written list of value and fruit of the Spirit words that you desire for your family. If you're married, you and your spouse should be in agreement about these words.

With these two tasks completed, you now have the beginnings of your family vision statement. When we got to this point, we could see a couple of words more clearly that ultimately became a significant part of our family's vision. One was that our family loved to entertain (at least that's what we called it at the time). We loved to have people over, and Danielle relished spending all day getting ready by cleaning the house and cooking. As we poured over our list of words, *hospitable* popped out at us. We defined the word, which we've done for you in Appendix B, so we understood clearly what it meant, and then we agreed that we wanted our home to be a place of hospitality. We also wanted to teach our children how to be hospitable, so the word is still on our list and part of our vision statement.

Over time, hospitality has remained important to our family vision, but it has undergone a shift. Once we more truly understood what hospitality meant, our preparation changed. Also, as our children got older, they contributed more to the preparation and the hospitality.

One Sunday we invited some dear friends to come over for the evening. Our whole family spent the afternoon preparing for this visit. We did not spend much time deep cleaning the house like we once did; superficial clutter clearing and a quick dusting was all we considered necessary. Next, we prayed for the family that was heading our way and for each other. This has become a great part of our hospitality and we have seen amazing results. Finally, our teenagers decided to put together a menu that included chicken cordon bleu that Noah knew how to prepare from working at a grocery store. They went to the store for all the ingredients and then spent the next hour together preparing the somewhat elaborate fare.

As we shared the meal with the other family, we enjoyed the contribution everyone had made for the event. Hospitality is an obvious ingredient in our family vision because in the bigger picture it brings our family joy and unity while blessing others. Hospitality is not important to our family only because we like to cook together but because we love to serve, show affection to others, and make them feel welcome. It is great fun.

The other word we included in our list was *honor*. This was always an important word in our house, but it lacked real meaning until we went through this process. We remember telling our children several times when we saw them not honoring that they needed to honor one another. The problem, we learned, was that we were assuming they knew what it meant and what the evidence would be if they were doing it.

Now, when we see our kids acting honorably, we praise them for it and talk about how we as a family are living in more honor. The point for all of us was that if we can model this in our home, it's easier for us to take honor and other vision words into the world and show the love of God to others. Honoring one another is a big part of living out the Gospel.

> Be devoted to one another in love. Honor one another above yourselves.
> (Romans 12:10, *AMP*)

As you develop your list, start thinking and talking about how you will intentionally teach and transfer these words and values to your children. With any good vision there will be a mission to complete or an action that needs to be done. In fact, now is a good time to consider the actions you need to take to live a life according to the value words you and your spouse have agreed upon. It is this action and intentionality that will provide the fuel to move you forward in the vision for your family. Without action, these words are just that; words.

For example, if *peaceful* is a value word for your family, consider the evidence of peace:

- Knowing God is in control
- Staying out of conflicts
- Feeling safe
- Free to live for Christ
- Calmness in the midst of difficult situations

How do you get to a place of living in peace? You intentionally look past the present circumstances and keep focused on your vision goals. You forgive other family members when they fall short of the values you have decided upon and encourage them to return to those values. When a family member demonstrates the evidence of peace, you acknowledge and congratulate that success. Instead of allowing external forces to drive peace away when unsettling news arrives, redirect your focus to knowing that God is in control. Practicing these intentional responses will become easier over time, and eventually they will simply become your supernatural response.

Another example of a word that came alive for us during this process is *generosity*. We wanted to intentionally help our children understand the joy that comes from giving generously. On my way home from work one day I went to the bank and took out some cash that we had been saving for this adventure with the kids.

We called a family meeting, and I told the kids I had something I wanted to give them. I counted out the money from the bank envelope on the table so the kids could see and then pushed it toward them. We watched their eyes widen. We told them that this money was for them, but there were two conditions if they accepted it.

First, they could not consume it, meaning they could not save it or spend it on themselves or one another. The second condition was that they had to tell us what they would do with it. It was only after a few seconds that the kids understood. Nathan said, "So we need to give it away, right?" We agreed; it was the only option.

The kids agreed to the conditions, took the money, and went into the boys' room to discuss what they would do with it. It took them about forty-five minutes before they were ready to give us an account of what they had decided to do. We were overwhelmed with what we heard next.

They had all thought it through and agreed upon how the money should be distributed. That in itself was terrific, but the most overwhelming part was hearing to whom and what they were going to give the money. They began going down the list in detail as to why they chose this person or that organization. We heard a couple of names of kids we didn't even know who had a need. One kid needed shoes, and our kids wanted to provide a pair for this boy.

After the explanation, we took each amount and put it in a separate envelope with each name or organization on it and drove the kids around to let them give the money away. We instructed them to say, "This is a blessing from the Lord we want to give to you," and that was all.

As we drove them around, we watched the kids go to the people and organizations on the list. Each time the kids ran back to the car with such great joy on their faces because they had chosen to bless others with this gift. They got it. They gave a gift, and they received the joy of giving.

This example should give you an understanding of how action toward your value words will result in many victories for your family. It may be helpful at this time to review your lists of words, summarize an action for each one, and intentionally formalize a plan for implementation. Refer to Appendices A and B to determine the evidence of each value.

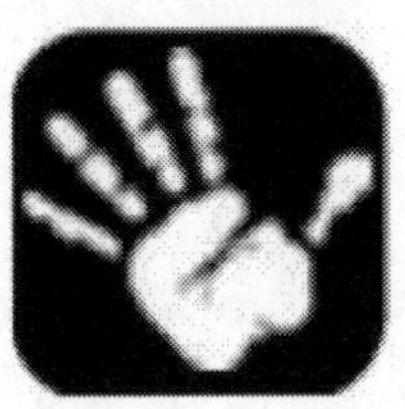

Reflection: Please turn to the accompanying workbook before you move on.

Five

Asking Your Kids To Help

THE FIRST STEPS TO INVOLVE YOUR CHILDREN

Now you're ready to intentionally ask the kids to be involved in the process. The steps you've taken so far have been written in a specific order for a purpose. It's important for you, as parents, to complete your steps before you call your first family meeting. If you're prepared, this will go well and you will see how God will move your family quickly into this great vision as soon as the kids are involved.

The next steps to developing your family vision statement can be fun as well as helpful for you as parents. One very important lesson we've learned in helping families is that the kids want to be included. They want a voice in the family. More important, they want to know that you as a family are going somewhere. They want to know there are higher mountains to climb and greater peaks to be reached. They want to be on the adventure with you. As we illustrated in Chapter 1, children are very good at imagining adventures. We want them to have something real and tangible to see, feel, and do. This process begins with what we call "setting the table" for honesty and transparency.

We talked about the guidelines at the table prior to our first meeting with the kids. These guidelines, listed in the following section, helped invite our children into the discussion. They allowed the kids to feel safe expressing themselves without any immediate feedback from us.

1. First, begin as a couple, or alone with the Lord, by praying for each of your children. Consider their individual gifts and how they bless the family as a whole. Space has been provided in the workbook to journal this step.

Reflection: Please turn to the accompanying workbook before you move on.

2. Tell your children that you need their help. You've set this time aside intentionally, and your children may already sense that something is going on. That's okay. If you have a tradition of family meetings, they may think this is just another one of those. It is, of course, a family meeting, but set the environment to be one of positive expectations. This is not the time to bring up any negative issues.

3. Explain that you've been working on the family vision and define that for them. A family vision statement will give your family something greater to focus on and move toward. Tell them you want to go on a great adventure and you want to take them with you. Assure them that you desire their input.
4. Refrain from sharing the words you've already chosen to describe your family until they have contributed their own words. Ask them to describe the family as others might see it, as they desire it to be, and maybe even how God sees it.
5. Now comes the difficult part: Do not respond or react to what happens next. Encourage them to continue by asking them what other words come to their minds. Praise them for the words they contribute and write them down. If necessary, refresh the question but continue to refrain from any judgment. We cannot overemphasize the importance of this step.

Visit www.c2family.com/videos and watch the *Involving the Kids* video for more coaching.

Discovering how your children describe your family can be very encouraging. Consider their words thoughtfully. Their descriptions will reflect their level of maturity and should be encouraged accordingly. For example, if your three-year-old uses the word *fun,* that's wonderful. Write it down and thank him or her for the contribution. When your teenager uses a simple word, accept it as well, but encourage a deeper explanation that reveals greater perception. Your sixteen-year-old may use the word *peaceful*. Consider drawing her out by saying, "What do you mean by that?" Whatever they say is okay. Write it down, and consider what they're trying to communicate. Thank them for being honest, and continue.

We understand that for some families this simple exercise can be a bit of a thought explosion. If your teenagers have become disrespectful as a result of their environment, peers, and the media, they may take advantage of the carte blanche nature of the discussion. Remember, this is not the time for judgment or anger. Accept their comments as they may test you to see just how much freedom you are allowing. Write their words down, and refrain from giving them "the look." As time proves your commitment to your family's vision, they will begin to see a difference and may retract some of their less than positive comments. This is not the final step in the process of becoming a supernatural family. It is, in many cases, your first step in reintroducing honor, respect, and values.

Many victories will be accomplished through this simple exercise. Not only do you have a description of your family on which everyone agrees, you also have words and values that your family wants to work toward—together. Inevitably, as you and your family discuss how God might describe you, you are already developing a vision of who you want to become.

Permit time for the discussion to fully develop, and then allow it to wind down on its own. Sometimes it's toward the end of the conversation that the children finally feel free and comfortable enough to share their heart about your family. You've been preparing for this for four chapters, and they may be just beginning to realize what's going on. Your family is becoming supernatural!

CONSIDER YOUR CHILDREN

As the family vision conversation winds down, take this opportunity to really consider your children. *Considering* is spiritual and requires putting them first, listening, and asking the Lord to show you something you can't see or hear naturally. When we listen to our kids and they tell us something from their hearts, we pause because we want to first understand and hear from the Lord. We silently pray for the Lord to give us clarity, understanding, revelation, or a picture to consider. Why do we want to consider our children? Look at this verse.

> And let us consider and give attentive, continuous care to watching over one another, studying how we may stir up (stimulate and incite) to love and helpful deeds and noble activities. (Hebrews 10:24, *AMP*)

By considering our kids, we are able to respond in a way that will bring about love, forgiveness, healing—whatever is the best response—because we love them and want more for them, and we want to know their hearts.

Once you've heard their words and written them down, it's a good time to read the words back to them like this: "Cori, you said *different*, meaning you like that we are a *different* family. That's awesome. Noah, your words were *honor, joy,* and *patient*. Great words. Nathan, you said, *hospitality, caring,* and *compassionate.* Wow, we love that these are words you use to describe our family." Now your children know you've listened. You might say, "You all are so awesome and have been very helpful to us today. We really appreciate your help." Whatever you say, be sincere.

As you review the words, you may find that many of them are also on the list of words agreed upon by you and your spouse. That is wonderful. If there are words from your list that you feel need to be introduced, now is the time to share them. Be careful that you use them as additional contributions to the process with ample explanation so the kids still sense the importance of their participation. They should rally around the new words and be excited to include them.

When an exhaustive list of words and descriptions of your family has been completed, explain to the family that you will take all the words and incorporate them into a paragraph or two that will become the vision for the family. Be sure you tell them that once they have been compiled into a readable format, you will reconvene later to get their feedback. It is very important that you conduct a second family meeting regarding the vision statement. In fact, it may take more than two, depending on the ages of your children, to come into complete agreement on the wordsmithing of value words, fruit of the Spirit words, and descriptions of what your family is aspiring to become.

START, STOP, CONTINUE (SSC)

I spent many years in the corporate world helping family businesses build their leadership teams. Through the years our group facilitated many corporate team-building experiences, and I learned a lot about people and how to build teams. I want to share something from the corporate world that we have used in helping families become more intentional and ultimately experience the supernatural power God has planned for them. We call this step "Start, Stop, and Continue," and there is space provided in the workbook to complete it as well as revisit this very helpful exercise in the future.

Before you dismiss the kids from the table you might say something like this as you begin the next step: "Hey, guys, before you go we want to ask you a few quick questions, and whatever your answers are we appreciate them, and it's okay to share your honest thoughts. So here's the first question. As a family, what things should we *start* doing that we are not doing now?"

This will tell you volumes about what they believe your family should be doing to become more like the family they envision or desire. We've had answers such as, "We want to go on family mission trips, camping, a family reunion," and so on. We encourage them, thank them, and write down their answers without any response.

Don't be surprised by what they say. Some children will give answers that define how a family looks to them because they have seen other families model certain behaviors or activities. One father told us that one of his children said she wanted to start having a family movie night because she had a friend whose family did this on a regular basis. If you consider this deeply, it will begin to show you what your kids believe is a healthy family. What they are really saying is that they have seen fruit or evidence in other families, and they want the same for theirs. It is really good to listen to them as they metaphorically paint a picture of a healthy family.

The next question we ask is, "As a family, what things should we *stop* doing? This may be for the family as a whole, or it can even be specific to us—Mom or Dad. Whatever it is, it's okay to tell us."

When we first asked this question we really weren't prepared for what happened next. Remember, at this point your children have trusted you because you've allowed them to talk without a negative response, so they may feel they can truly speak from their hearts without ducking. Again, listen and don't respond except with encouragement and thankfulness.

Many parents have expressed a wish to us, "if I could only know what my kids are thinking." Here you go. You are giving them permission to be honest and transparent about the family and about you as parents. This may just be the beginning of the great conversations you've been longing to have with your children. We have listed a few of the responses we've heard from other parents, some who were a little shocked, but they all said, "We were glad to get this out in the open."

- "We wish our family would stop using degrading smack talk."
- "I wish you both would get to know some of the other parents from my school. You always just leave after the event or the game."
- "Dad, I would like for you to stop cussing."
- "We wish you would stop smoking."
- "We wish you would stop arguing."
- "Dad, we wish you were home more."
- "Mom, you're always on your phone."

Okay, I'm sure you get an idea of where this may go. The truth is, they're already thinking it, and what you've done is allowed them to say what's on their minds without responding to them immediately. Whatever you think you want to say, *don't*! Let them talk—just listen.

The dad who shared the story about his cussing told me he didn't even know he swore. He said that he listened and quietly considered what his children said without an immediate response. After the family meeting he asked his wife about it, and she told him, "Well, darling, sometimes you're in the shop and drop a tool or something, and you do get pretty 'colorful'. Your kids hear it all over the yard."

This dad had just learned something, and after talking to his wife and considering what his kids had said, he responded a few days later by first asking for forgiveness and then promising to be a better example. After this, he thanked them for having the courage to tell him and hugged them.

Wow! Can you imagine how his kids felt? They were a part of a family moving toward something greater. They had a voice, and it mattered. Can you see what happened here? Do you think those kids will use curse words after their dad's response? What they didn't realize is that they learned about a family value and its importance.

I remember one year when we asked our children this question, we didn't get a response from our daughter until days later when Danielle and I were alone with her on the way to church. She said out of nowhere, "Dad, I have an answer to the question."

I said, "What question?"

"You know, the one about us as a family, what we would like to stop doing."

"Oh," I said, "that question. Yes, go on." She went on to tell me how I acted in restaurants when the person who was waiting on our family didn't give me the service I wanted or expected. She said it was really embarrassing.

"You know that one time when you couldn't find our waiter, and you went into the kitchen to find him? That was really horrifying. And that one time when I had my friend Madison with me, and you yelled across the room to your waitress who forgot your butter? I just wanted to crawl under the table." She went on and on. I had no idea what a jerk I'd been in front of my daughter and how she perceived me in these situations. I really learned a lot about myself, and it took the courage of a twelve-year-old to tell me.

After I carefully listened, I finally said, "Wow, Cori, thank you for sharing that with me. It really means a lot, and I want to consider it for a day or two and talk to your mom. I promise to get back to you soon. Is that okay?"

"Sure, Dad," she replied. When we got out of the car, I hugged her and thanked her again for having the courage to tell me what was in her heart.

Later that afternoon, when I brought it up to Danielle, it didn't take long for her to confirm that I sometimes acted like a spoiled brat who wanted special treatment. After I considered the conversation some more, I realized that because I was paying for a service and didn't get it, I felt justified in my behavior. But what Cori was saying was that I may have been justified by the world's standards, but if you want to be a family that is different from the world, you have to respond differently. She was right, and I am so thankful she had the courage to bring it to my attention.

A few days later, when Cori was at home, I asked her, "Hey, girl, do you have a few minutes?" She did, and with her mom in the room I told her, "You know, Cori, I really considered what you told me in the car about how I act sometimes in restaurants, and you are so right. In fact, I can see how my behavior embarrassed you, and I want to ask you to forgive me."

"Of course, Dad," she said. Again we hugged, and I thanked her.

Now when we're in a restaurant and I'm not getting the service I expect, I just look over at Cori, and we both smile. She sees God in me in giving the wait staff grace and showing kindness. That's what they really deserve. Cori again saw a change that led to a more Godly example of her family. We all learned something through this, especially me.

The reason I had Danielle in the room was because Cori had told that story to both of us on the way to church, and I wanted her to know we had discussed it and were in agreement. If Cori had brought that up to me when we were alone, I still would have talked about it with Danielle, but I would have approached Cori alone because that's how she had come to me.

Another thing we learned from this encounter was that Cori was demonstrating our family value 'honor'. She had used discernment and patience by waiting until an opportune time to answer the question of what she would like to see stop. Cori honored me as her father. Now, we laugh about it when we are all out as a family and we share it with others but the first confrontation was handled with respect by our daughter.

The last question is, "As a family, what things should we *continue* to do?" Here it is, the confirmation of what you're doing well as parents and as a family. Write these down as well and be thankful for whatever they have to say. Also know that this will become the longest list over time as you become more intentional and move into your vision.

The reason it's the last question is because it ends the process on a very positive note. Again, thank them, and let them know you will get back together after you have begun the vision statement, and you need time to consider what they have told you. Hug them, and tell them you love them.

This is some of what our kids have said to us when we ask this question.

- We want to continue going on family mission trips (now with much more specifics).
- We want to continue to have other families over for our monthly family gatherings (they are now inviting other families).

- We want to have our extended family at our house for holidays (so they can help prepare and serve).
- We want to continue to go camping (they love the memories).
- We want to continue to love and encourage one another (because we need one another).

Let us encourage you. You may get to this question and all you hear is crickets. No one has anything to say. The good news is, as you develop your vision statement and become intentional in living it out, you will see an amazing supernatural difference in only one year. You will see much fruit from your children and in your family.

What we have heard from our kids in their responses to this question tells us that we are seeing fruit by intentionally passing Godly values to our children. Why do we know this? It's because we see the evidence in the decisions they make and the way they live their lives. It's what we all want as parents, confirmation that we are making a difference in the outcome for our families. This is intentionally creating a legacy that will last for generations; now our children will pass these values to their children.

Over the years as this has developed in our family, we have even seen our kids make intentional decisions about school, careers, and how or where they will serve, with what and whom they will be involved, and so on because of these values instilled in them. We have also watched our older kids become great, intentional, Godly parents, bear much fruit in their families, and help other families by their example. We continue to encourage them all to live supernaturally and abundantly and fulfill the purpose for which God created them. Our decision of being intentional has now allowed us to watch our children grow up into intentional young adults and parents. Now, as our act of continuous stewardship in this process, we want to help them, with our five grandchildren, do the same.

Reflection: Please turn to the accompanying workbook before you move on.

Six

God's Greater Purpose

God created your family for a purpose. As you receive His vision for your family, it is important that you understand His purpose. It took us many years to understand God's purpose for our family. We want others to learn from our story. We were good at living the natural life. I had a good career, I made a good living, and I had a beautiful family. From the world's perspective, we were doing it right. We were living the American Dream, but God never said, "Go forth and live the American Dream." In fact, we found that God gave us a bigger charge. Let's look at the first chapter of Genesis. Not only did God give us a charge, He also gave us everything we would need to accomplish that charge because He made us in His likeness and in His image.

Look closely at the words He spoke in Genesis, Chapter 1, verses you have most likely read or heard many times.

> God said, Let Us [Father, Son, and Holy Spirit] **make** mankind **in Our image**, after **Our likeness**, and let them have complete **authority** over the fish of the sea, the birds of the air, the [tame] beasts, and over all of the earth, and over everything that creeps upon the earth. So God created man in His own image, in the image and likeness of God He created him; male and female He created them. And **God blessed** them and said to them, be **fruitful**, **multiply**, and **fill the earth**, and **subdue** it [using all its vast resources in the service of God and man]; and have **dominion** over the fish of the sea, the birds of the air, and over every living creature that moves upon the earth.
> (Genesis 1:26–28, *AMP*; emphasis added)

Do you see something new in the words spoken when God created us? They were not just a pat on the back and "good luck." God gave us these words to go and live a life of adventure and abundance with authority. Before He gave us this charge, He did something that shows how much He loves us and how important our lives and destinies are on this earth: He blessed us.

Blessed; Set apart, consecrated (declared sacred), adored.

With this charge God demonstrated His affection for the created likeness and image of Himself by saying to us we are special, very special. More specifically, He set us apart from all other creation, declared us sacred and adored us. That's pretty special. So now lets look further into these words in the verses above.

God's family created family! (Father, Son, Holy Spirit)

- Make (fashioned together like only a Creator can do)
- He gave us complete authority (power)
- In His Image (represent—literally to re-present again)
- Likeness (similar)
- Fruitful (to live in fruitfulness/abundance)
- Multiply (the abundance)
- Fill (fulfill a purpose and produce more of His image and likeness)
- Subdue (overcome the world)
- Dominion (reign over)

In these words we see a supernatural purpose for family. Supernatural because with out his ordaining (speaking into existence) the order of things created and how they would function it would not be so. It was only from His supernatural order we were set apart.

The One who created us did so in particular order. His order illustrated our dominion over the other creation and the purpose He had in that dominion. We understood this passage in a different light once we understood that God had a purpose for our family and in all families. Further evidence to the purpose of family can be seen in the Old Testament genealogies. Family is important to God. He created family to love, worship, disciple, and be the Gospel. And as only the Creator can do, He demonstrated His purpose for each family from the charge above.

GOD CREATED FAMILY TO DEMONSTRATE HIS LOVE

Families were created for a purpose. When we look at God's creation of man, in His image and in His likeness, we see His purpose. The evidence of this is how God demonstrates His love through family. God's love is a supernatural love. It's a love that knows no boundaries, is unconditional, and is always contending for a greater purpose until that greater purpose becomes a present tense reality.

This supernatural love is manifested effortlessly in a family who seeks God's greater reward. When every one of our children was born and put into our arms, we immediately loved him or her. We loved our children unconditionally, with no boundaries, and we will always contend for their greater good. This love is supernatural. We didn't have to get to know the child by waiting to see how things would go, what his or her personality would be like, or what actions he or she would take. It didn't matter. We supernaturally loved each of them from the start.

No matter what our children do or don't do, we love them. Our love for our children is unconditional. We may not always like the choices they make, but we will contend for them until the right behavior and destiny are achieved. It's the same with other members of our extended family. We love them and want them all to know of our love and God's purpose for the family.

God is the same with you and me. He loved us when He formed us. He knew us then, He knows us now and He continues to love us unconditionally. He is always contending for us for a greater purpose, which is the destiny He designed for us. Once we understood this kind of love and where it came from, knowing that it was a supernatural demonstration of God's love for us, we began to understand that we were to take this love out into the world as well.

God demonstrates His love for us, created us in His image and in His likeness to be fruitful and multiply this fruit throughout the world. What did Jesus say is the greatest commandment?

> "Teacher, which is the greatest commandment in the Law?" Jesus replied: "'Love the Lord your God with all your heart and with all your soul and with all your mind.'
> [38] This is the first and greatest commandment.
> [39] And the second is like it: 'Love your neighbor as yourself.'
> [40] All the Law and the Prophets hang on these two commandments." (Matthew 22:36–40, AMP)

By living in the fruit of the Spirit, Jesus said that the greatest of these is love. It is this supernatural love that we are to take into the world, the love demonstrated to us by God through our family. What if I made a choice to treat all of God's people who, by the way were also created in His image and in His likeness, with this type of love? Unconditional, while contending for each person with whom God brings us into a relationship. Would that not be fulfilling His purpose, demonstrating the love of Heaven here on earth?

His purpose really comes down to a simple multiplication of His love demonstrated through our families, Love God, love people unconditionally while contending for the best possible outcome until it becomes a present tense reality. So be it!

GOD CREATED FAMILY TO WORSHIP

The second reason God created family is because we were created to worship Him and worship Him only.

> Jesus answered, "It is written: 'Worship the Lord your God and serve him only.'" (Luke 4:8, *AMP*)

How does my family worship? There are several ways we intentionally worship our Creator, and, as it turns out, God gave us the ability to do all of these things by living in the fruit of the Spirit. God sent us His Spirit for us to have all we need in order to live and manifest this fruit. We worship Him by the way we choose to live in the abundance of His Spirit and by believing this abundance is for us. It's the relationship with His Spirit that brings about this supernatural fruit in our lives.

Now that we see this supernatural fruit in our families, how can we *not* worship with a heart of praise and thanksgiving? If your family had this supernatural love, joy, peace, and the other fruit found in Galatians 5:22, would you not also be overjoyed, praising Him always, and thanking Him continuously for loving you so much?

Another way we worship is through our obedience to living intentionally as His disciples and teaching our children to be disciples.

Being intentional takes leadership, and leadership begins with a change in our own hearts and willingness to become more like our Creator. This change is the essence of leadership. You will not change your family, others, organizations, or cultures effectively without first having a change from within your own heart that will bring about His greater purpose.

To become disciples, we must first be willing to be disciplined as the leaders of our families so we can know and then live out the truth as an example to our families. Notice how the words *disciple* and *discipline* are very similar. They both have a purpose to bring about a change in one's heart and actions with intentionality. Here is how *Merriam-Webster* defines discipline:

1. punishment
2. instruction
3. a field of study
4. training that corrects, molds, or perfects the mental faculties or moral character
5. control gained by enforcing obedience or order or orderly or prescribed conduct or pattern of behavior or self-control
6. a rule or system of rules governing conduct or activity

Look at how God defines discipline in these verses.

> **24** Do you not know that in a race all the runners compete, but [only] one receives the prize? So run [your race] that you may lay hold [of the prize] *and* make it yours.

25 Now every athlete who goes into training conducts himself temperately *and* restricts himself in all things. They do it to win a wreath that will soon wither, but we [do it to receive a crown of eternal blessedness] that cannot wither.
26 Therefore I do not run uncertainly (without definite aim). I do not box like one beating the air *and* striking without an adversary.
27 But [like a boxer] I buffet my body [handle it roughly, discipline it by hardships] and subdue it, for fear that after proclaiming to others the Gospel *and* things pertaining to it, I myself should become unfit [not stand the test, be unapproved and rejected as a counterfeit].
(1 Corinthians 9:24–27, *AMP*)

11 For the grace of God has appeared that offers salvation to all people.
12 It teaches us to say "No" to ungodliness and worldly passions, and to live self-controlled, upright and godly lives in this present age,
13 while we wait for the blessed hope—the appearing of the glory of our great God and Savior, Jesus Christ,
14 who gave himself for us to redeem us from all wickedness and to purify for himself a people that are his very own, eager to do what is good. (Titus 2:11–14, *AMP*)

You then, my son, be strong in the grace that is in Christ Jesus.

> **2** And the things you have heard me say in the presence of many witnesses entrust to reliable people who will also be qualified to teach others.
> **3** Join with me in suffering, like a good soldier of Christ Jesus.
> **4** No one serving as a soldier gets entangled in civilian affairs, but rather tries to please his commanding officer.
> **5** Similarly, anyone who competes as an athlete does not receive the victor's crown except by competing according to the rules.
> **6** The hardworking farmer should be the first to receive a share of the crops. (2 Timothy 2:1–6, *AMP*)

A true disciple of Jesus is one who is not just a hearer of the word but also a doer of the word. We worship the Lord as we practice the things of God through becoming intentional in our own training and Godly behavior toward our families and others.

It wasn't long ago that Danielle and I had to work specifically on training ourselves, through discipline, in order to train and disciple our children. God gave this responsibility to us—not our church, our school, or others. When we are intentional and do these things He has asked us to do, it's truly an act of worship.

GOD CREATED FAMILY TO DISCIPLE

Family is the training ground for God's truths to be taught and demonstrated. Parents are given the responsibility to disciple their children to seek the Lord, and through their example illustrate a life of living for God. Discipleship is simply training through example and correction.

> Train up a child in the way he should go, even when he is old he will not depart from it. (Proverbs 22:6, *NASB*)

This verse is important because it truly implies intentionality. Let's break it down and understand what these words mean and how we are to apply them to our families.

First, *train up* is a purposeful element of parenting. When we begin any training, it's normally with an idea of a desired outcome. When you invest your time and resources in training, it is to achieve a level of completion or become a master of something.

Even people in today's society seek training. It contains the expectation of reaching a specific level of accomplishment to achieve a desired outcome. Someone had to have developed and implemented a plan for this training for these outcomes to attain reality.

The verse continues, *in the way he should go*. In which way do we want our children to go? What does this look like? What we are after is the desired outcome for each of our children individually. The outcome desired here is, the fruit in Galatians 5:22–23 that is produced from training and helping each child to live out his or her individual purpose or destiny. In other words, *in the way Noah should go, in the way Nathan should go, in the way Cori should go,* and so on. Because each child is unique and has individual gifts, talents, and anointings, we are simply training them up for God's greater purpose in the way they individually should go. We are coming alongside what God has already instilled in each child and, as described in 2 Timothy, Chapter 1, fanning it into the gift of God. The training will be different for each child even though the desired outcome is the same—living abundantly in the fruit of the Spirit.

The rest of the verse is also the result of the manifested fruit of the child: *When he gets old he won't depart from it.* Old? Do we have to wait until our children get old to see if this training will stick, that they haven't departed from it? The way *old* is used here does not necessarily refer to age but to a level of spiritual maturity.

If we had a spiritual maturity chart, it would look like this:

Stage	**Derivation**	**Definition**
birth	conversion	spiritually born again
infants	nepios (Latin)	childish, untaught
children	paidion (Latin)	young child, simpleminded
young adult	teknon (Greek)	Adolescent, becoming independent
mature adult	huois (Greek)	fully mature, beloved
perfected (old)	telios (Greek)	complete, lacking nothing

(Weaver 279-298)

The word old really means to have reached spiritual maturity. At what age does this take place? It depends. You are uniquely qualified to train up your children because God gave them to *you* and not some other set of parents. We believe that even adoption situations are ordained by God, so the same rule applies. Be confident that you are the right parents for your children, and seek the Holy Spirit's guidance.

Your vision statement is an important part of this training up. It should be fun and creative, not a burden. There are many other practical tools for fulfilling God's purpose for training your families in our online course at www.c2family.com. As you become successful in living out this purpose, you will begin to help disciple other families as well.

To simplify this further, we as parents must be disciplined in our own life to be like Jesus. We must do our best to think, talk and act as Jesus did. Being a great disciple is really just being the example for our children to see and know what it looks like to be "One of His disciples" by the way we live our life.

Now as a family, we can go into the world (maybe it's your neighborhood, or apartment complex) and be an example or a disciple to others. Our task here on earth is to make disciples. First, this starts with our family. Then we simply invite others into our life to see the example of what a disciple of Jesus looks like and because God created them also in His image and in His likeness they will want to know Him more because of your example.

GOD CREATED FAMILY TO BE THE GOSPEL

God created our families to be the light of the world. When Jesus said, "by their fruits you will know them," He meant that by their life, by their demonstration of God's love and living in the abundance of the supernatural fruit, they were disciples—they would stand out to the world.

> Therefore by their fruits you will know them. (Matthew 7:20, *NKJV*)

By living as God created us to live in the abundance of His supernatural fruit, and by demonstration of His love to one another, we are the Gospel. Our families are the Good News that Jesus lived and died for. God sent His Son to redeem what was lost when Adam and Eve ate of the forbidden fruit, and before Jesus died He told his disciples that it was good for Him to go so through His Spirit we could do yet greater things than even He did.

> Truly, truly, I say to you, he who believes in Me, the works that I do, he will do also; and greater works than these he will do; because I go to the Father. (John 14:12, *NASB*)

And greater things you will do! You may already be experiencing this greatness. When we made the decision to become intentional and seek God's vision for our family, it did not take long for the evidence to become real. In fact, even before we realized what was happening, God was showing us the supernatural. On our first family mission trip, greater works took place than we could have imagined in our wildest dreams. While installing safe stoves and fixing leaky roofs in a small community in Guatemala, Bill was working side by side with two of our boys and an interpreter when he sprayed a toxic tarlike material and it hit his eyes. He immediately bent over, blinded. He took his shirt off to wipe his eyes. The interpreter, Christopher, silently read the warning label: "Rinse with clean water for fifteen minutes and seek professional help immediately." Great, they had less than three ounces of clean water left in Noah's water bottle and the nearest "professional" was hours away. Christopher began to call on the name of Jesus. Bill could not see, and there was a putrid black goo oozing from both eyes. As our sons began to help Bill return to our base, they all prayed for healing. At the creek crossing, Christopher asked if Bill could see. Bill raised his head for the first time and said everything was very blurry. Christopher looked skyward and said, "Blurry, is not good enough, Jesus, heal this man!"

With the confidence of a seasoned pastor this seventeen-year-old called on the name of our Savior, and Bill was healed. When he reached the rest of us, he could see. None of us knew the extent of the danger until the last night of the trip. We took the team to a restaurant in Guatemala City where we would meet Christopher's parents. The meeting was quite emotional as Christopher conveyed the danger of the chemical reaction and said, "I knew all we had was Jesus, and all we needed was Jesus!" We will never forget the experience, and Noah and Nathan saw their first verifiable miracle! Since then we have had the courage to expect great things. You see, greater things can happen every day and in every country; we just need the courage and expectation to realize them.

Sometimes the "greater things" we get to be a part of involve watching other families recapture their dreams, realize their purpose, receive their vision, and create their legacy. We are watching the culture change, one family at a time, and we feel that that is a great gift.

Can you see how powerful this is for all of us? We have everything we need to live abundantly, free, with the authority and the power to overcome even the world.

What if others see something in you they do not fully understand? What if they say to you, "Whatever it is you all have, I want for my family," and they mean it? By their fruits you will know them, right? What if you help just a few other families understand this supernatural power of family so they, too, can walk fully in it? What if they, in turn, do the same? Could we not win back our streets, our apartment complexes, our cul-de-sacs, our towns and cities? Even the world?

God created your family for a greater purpose, and now you have the vision to go and live in it. You will become an agent of change in this generation and for generations to come. It begins with your family, but it doesn't stop there.

How do we change the culture? One family at a time! How do we bring Heaven to earth? One family at a time! You are the next family!

FINAL STEPS

If you've read this book and followed each intentional step, you should already be seeing real fruit in your family because of your experience in developing vision, getting into agreement, and looking forward to involving the kids. You are becoming intentional.

You've taken tangible steps that will change the outcome for your family now and possibly for generations to come. This is a huge deal. Because of your willingness to be intentional and not leave your family to chance, you've done what others may not be willing to do. You've tilled the soil for your family and begun a process for planting seeds through the ongoing intentional steps of making your vision a present tense reality. You will see a harvest of blessings.

There is only one more step to take to complete your first vision statement. For many of you this last step may be the biggest blessing. Take the words, phrases, and lists, all of them, and begin to wordsmith them together to form your vision statement with prayer and guidance from the Holy Spirit. You began with words that were only yours, and then you added words as a couple, then you convened as a family and added words, phrases, and ideas as a team. You have all the ingredients you need to create your actual vision statement. Pray for the Holy Spirit to be a part of this process as He was in all the others. Take your time and let the words flow into a beautiful picture of who your family is becoming. Remember, this is your first, but it will not be your last. Over time you will return to these steps, renew your vision, and receive deeper revelation. We recommend revisiting your vision statement with your family on an annual basis. Your vision most likely will not change, but you will gain new meaning and a more intrinsic understanding as time goes by.

You've successfully written your vision on the tablet of your heart, meaning it's planted deep inside your spirit and important to your family. Like it says in Proverbs 3:3 (*CEB*),

> Don't let loyalty and faithfulness leave you. Bind them on your neck; write them on the tablets of your heart.

Be proud of what you've accomplished. As with all great undertakings, you should show your family and friends the work you're proud of by displaying your vision statement where everyone can see it. Go ahead, display it where others, especially your family, can see it often. As it says in Habakkuk 2:2 (*CEB*),

Write a vision; make it plain on a tablet so that a runner can read it.

This may be your first attempt at a family vision statement, so keep in mind that it will evolve over time as your family reaches new levels for the Kingdom of God. Watch Him bring about a great harvest in your family as time rolls on.

Here are a few examples of what others have done to display their family vision statement in their home. These families have gone through the process and now proudly display their vision statement, creatively and uniquely, for others to witness.

One family told us that this process brought them closer together in a supernatural way. The older kids took the lead in crafting the statement, making sure the words were incorporated and the vision statement had a real flow. It also began a new tradition of family prayer. When they started the process at the family meeting involving the kids, dad and mom asked them to pray for the leading of the Holy Spirit, but at the end it was the children who asked for prayer to finish the vision statement.

For some of you, doing this may seem so far from where you are right now, but don't underestimate what God wants to do in your family and individually in your children.

Another family told us that the process of SSC became their vision. If they just did that over the next twelve months they would have great victory and abundant fruit. Now the whole family is focused on the things they decided to start, stop, and continue, and it has brought much-needed clarity and vision to a family that did not have a lot in common.

Remember the family whose dad said their house was nothing more than separate apartments? They had been living their lives exclusive of a greater purpose. Their vision statement took them on their first family mission trip, and now they are leading others in changing the world in Central America.

Look carefully at our family's vision statement. Note that we put in bold letters the words Danielle and I used from our list before we asked the kids for their words. These are the words on which we came into agreement, and they made it into the vision statement.

We are a different family. We love to be ***hospitable****, caring, and* ***helpful*** *toward our friends and our community. In all we* *do, we strive to be* ***passionate*** *in a loving and Godly way. As our passions define us, we desire to chase after God as we discover His gifts to us. We want to be first* ***prayerful,*** *then* ***intentional****, but flexible to remain hard working yet fun and active.*

We agree as a family to start eating better and camping; to stop arguing about stupid stuff and bringing up past mistakes. We want to continue mission work, serving at church, supporting our school, having meaningful talks, admitting our mistakes, and doing things together like traveling and sports.

Our family vision is to be good ***stewards*** *of all with which God has blessed us and* ***encourage*** *others through giving and* ***making a difference in the lives of families.***

The underlined words are the ones the kids gave us at our family meeting. They are now incorporated into the final written vision statement. What is significant and interesting about our family vision statement is this: our kids may not have our family vision statement memorized, but they know that each word they spoke back then is now represented in it. They provided input, and we listened. Our vision statement illustrates our joint family effort, and we all have to do our part to live it.

MULTIPLYING THE FRUIT

Now that you've written and displayed your family vision statement in your home, we want to prepare and help you. We want to prepare you because, as a result of your intentionality, other families will see something different about your family. Over time these families will want what you have. What God gives, He multiplies.

> Now He who supplies seed to the sower and bread for food will supply and multiply your seed for sowing and increase the harvest of your righteousness. (2 Corinthians 9:10, *NASB*)

People will ask you about your story and the process. They may even ask you for help. Be prepared to share your story and how you learned to become intentional using these very specific steps. This is where C2Family can come alongside you with your friends, a small group, or whoever you "do life" with, and help you encourage them to take the intentional steps for their family just as you did for yours.

To order additional copies of this book as a resource for others, visit our store at www.c2family.com. For a more in-depth guide through the steps of becoming an intentional family with a vision, we offer an online learning center. It's designed to be used by individual families or, better yet, a small group and includes much of the content from this book using a more hands-on approach. The online experience takes you deeper into the reasons to become intentional, encompasses more thorough guidance to help you get into agreement, and really conveys the importance of considering your children for their uniqueness. It also encourages you to compose intentional lists for each of your children.

In addition, you will learn about God's purpose for creating family and how your family can play its most important role in the story of the Gospel. Remember, this is a great opportunity to be the evidence of what God wants to do in each family. By your family's fruit alone, you will cause others to want more for their families, and your vision statement allows you and your children to share your story, which is your testimony. Through your changed family and your testimony, you will help others overcome.

> They triumphed over him by the blood of the Lamb and by the word of their testimony. (Revelation 12:11, *AMP*)

Congratulations, you have taken a step of courage and will receive strength from the Lord as you move closer to His purpose for your family. If you really want a different outcome, you have to continue to take action because there is so much at stake.

What's at stake are our children and the generations after them. Your children and our children are asking for parents who will lead them into an adventure. They want good over bad. They want a Godly heritage and stories to be told. It's up to us to take those steps.

It was only a few years ago that we felt the world was having a greater impact on our children than we were. We were afraid of what we were seeing, and we were concerned about the potential for real disaster in our family. We had become lost to the world by our own choices. God's promises are true. He says many times to His people, "Return to Me, and I will return to you." He's waiting.

> For if you return to the LORD, your brothers and your sons will find compassion before those who led them captive and will return to this land. For the LORD your God is gracious and compassionate, and will not turn His face away from you if you return to Him.
> (2 Chronicles 30:9, *NASB*)

We encourage you to not let this be just another book you read. Knowledge without action has no power. Take intentional time to work this out each day. Remember, you either decide to be intentional, or you make the decision to leave it to chance. It's never too late to lead your family into a Godly vision and intentionally create a legacy. It is also never too late to become the example for others around you. Families desperately need to see the evidence of something greater in you and your family. As you begin to fulfill the vision God has given your family, be prepared to share your story and encourage others to begin the journey to a supernatural family.

Sometimes we feel like we're the most unlikely authors, teachers, and speakers about family and parenting, but all of this is a fulfillment of God's promise to the Ford family, and He will fulfill His promises to your family as well.

We would like to hear your story about your family as you begin your journey of vision and intentionality. We have a special place on our website for you to send us your story Please share with us at www.c2family.com.

OUR PRAYER FOR YOUR FAMILY

Lord, we pray for each family that is desperate for you right now. We know you love the heart of a mom and a dad willing to fight. Right now, begin to equip them. You, Lord, are already waiting to take them into their destiny and on the adventure of a lifetime like only You can do.

Lord, as these parents step out in faith, give them supernatural courage, strength, and protection for attacks on their families. Lord, You know the names of each of their children and grandchildren born today and those who will be born in your image and in your likeness in the future. Bless them (set apart, consecrated, adored) so these children and future children will know you and make You known by the fruit and power that you give through your Spirit and your son, Jesus. Help us live in abundant life, free from the world's lies. We pray over each family for more of You, Lord, in the all-sufficient name of Jesus. So be it!

Reflection: Please turn to the accompanying workbook before you move on.

Appendix A

Fruit of the Spirit Definitions

Fruit	True Definition	Evidence	Source
Love	always contending for the highest possible good in every situation and relentlessly contending until it is a present tense reality	generosity, selflessness, patience, humility, not being easily offended	(Weaver, 2012)
Joy	cheerfulness and calm delight, being exceedingly glad and not foiled by circumstances	thankfulness, hopefulness, worshipfulness, living abundantly, knowing God's presence	Olive Tree Bible App
Peace	the tranquil state of a soul assured of its salvation through Christ, therefore fearing nothing	restored relationships, courage, obedience, absence of anxiety	Olive Tree Bible App

Patience	optimistic expectation, ability to persevere bravely in enduring misfortune and trouble	confidence in the future, ability to listen to the Holy Spirit, seeing God working in others	Olive Tree Bible App
Kindness	love manifest in actions, maintaining relationships through gracious aid in times of need	eagerness to serve, intentional acts of service, desiring to encourage others	Olive Tree Bible App
Goodness	virtue and benevolence, an intentional preference for right over wrong	seeing the best in others, easily making good choices	Olive Tree Bible App
Faithfulness	steadfastness in affection or allegiance, unstoppable conviction	boldness, courage, keeping promises, being available to others	Olive Tree Bible App
Gentleness	sweet reasonableness, with an absence of harshness, willing to compromise where no moral issue is at stake	influence, showing compassion	precetaustin.org/greek_word_studies1.htm
Self-control	mastery of one's desires and passions, temperance and chastity	pure lifestyle, health, consideration, achievement of goals	Olive Tree Bible App

Appendix B

Value Words and Definitions

amiable: having and displaying a friendly and pleasant manner

benevolent: well meaning and kind; philanthropic

confident: self-assured, level- headed

considerate: perceptive to others' needs

discerning: having and displaying good judgment; discriminating, perceptive

enthusiastic: filled with or marked by a strong excitement of feeling

excellent: eminently good, first class

faithful: steadfast in affection or allegiance, having unstoppable conviction

flexible: ready and capable to adapt to new, different, or changing requirements

forgiving: able to give up resentment graciously

friendly: showing kindly interest and goodwill

frugal: characterized by or reflecting economy in the use of resources

generous: characterized by a noble or forbearing spirit

gentle: free from harshness, sternness or violence, mild and humble, willing to yield

graceful: pleasing; full of objective favor toward others

good: virtuous and benevolent, intentionally prefers right over wrong

harmonious: seeking to establish peace with or among others

helpful: of service or assistance

honest: marked by free, forthright, and sincere expression

honorable: guided by a high sense of value, placing value where it is lacking

hospitable: characterized by having affection for strangers and going out of one's way to make them feel welcome

humble: not proud, haughty, arrogant, or assertive

idealistic: well versed in ideas; especially in their abstract or symbolic character

industrious: persistently active, zealous

integrity: firm adherence to a code of moral values, incorruptibility

intelligent: possessing high mental capacity; ability to understand well

joyful; cheerfully calm manner, not affected by circumstances

just: deals with others fairly

kind: manifesting love in actions, maintaining relationships through gracious aid in times of need

knowledgeable: well informed, able to retain information

loving: relentlessly contending for the highest possible good in every situation until it's a present tense reality (Weaver, 2012)

loyal: unswerving in allegiance; faithful to a cause, ideal or custom

magnanimous: exhibiting or suggesting a lofty and courageous spirit

merciful: compassionate, always willing to provide relief

moderate: avoiding extreme behavior or expressions, observing reasonable limits

modest: able to place a moderate estimate on one's abilities or worth

noble: very good and excellent

obedient: submissive to the restraint or command of authority

objective: dealing with facts or conditions as perceived without distortion by personal feelings, prejudices, or interpretations

patient: optimistically expectant, able to persevere bravely in enduring misfortune and trouble

peaceful: having the tranquil state of a soul assured of its salvation through Christ, therefore fearing nothing

persevering: the quality of undertaking duty in spite of counterinfluences, opposition, or discouragement

practical: evidence based not theoretical

prayerful: spiritually considerate

prudent: judicious, shows wisdom

pure: free from worldly vices

purposeful: know their God-given mandate

quiescent: possessing a state of tranquil repose; nonplused (Psalm 46:10)

reasonable: not extreme or excessive

reliable: firm; morally true or certain

respectful: able to offer a person your very best regard-less of their position or rank

responsible: able to answer for one's conduct and obligations

reverent: worshipful

righteous: acting in accord with divine or moral law

sacrificial: surrendered for the sake of something better

self-control: mastery over your desires and passions; temperance, chastity

steadfast: firmly fixed in place, immovable

tactful: having a keen sense of what to do or say in order to maintain good relations

teachable: apt and willing to learn

temperate: Well behaved; avoids extremes

thankful: conscious of benefit received

tolerant: bearing with others in love, eager to maintain unity

trustworthy: worthy of confidence

understanding: the ability to comprehend easily or sympathize; compassionate

valuable: having great importance

wise: possessing comprehensive insight into the ways and purposes of God

Bibliography

Ware, Bronnie. *The Top Five Regrets of the Dying: A Life Transformed by the Dearly Departing.* Carlsbad, CA: Hay House, 2012.

Weaver, Kevin. *Re_Orient.* Southlake: Feasible, 2012.

Resources

Parenting is tough. We don't want you to get stuck along the way, so here are some resources that helped us get back on track. We share them here as recommendations.

Freedom Ministries: Your church may offer support for issues of past wounds and generational issues. These ministries can be very helpful if you identify issues in you, as parents, that you see manifesting in your children.

Weekend Retreats: These are for individual healing. If you find yourselves, as parents, unable to get past issues from your own childhood or even past relationships, a weekend retreat such as a Fellowship of the Sword Quest or Heartquest may be helpful. www.fellowshipofthesword.com.

Marriage is tough, too. If you find yourselves at an impasse, you may need to put the vision statement on hold and explore some of these helpful resources before you continue:

A Weekend to Remember: Get a way with your spouse to focus on each other and your marriage http://www.familylife.com/events.

Books that were helpful in our journey:

The Bondage Breaker by Neil T. Anderson
Raising Lambs among Wolves by Mark I. Bubeck

The Blessing by John Trent and Gary Smalley

Think Differently Live Differently by Bob Hamp

The Best Advice I Ever Got on Marriage compiled by Jim Daly

About the Author

For over sixteen years Bill has worked with families to help direct both wealth and values to the next generation. While many of the families he has worked with were broken and lacked the power and vision God intended, Bill and Danielle discovered their lives into a blended family also was living in spiritual poverty in need of freedom and truth as revealed in their first book, *The Power of Family Vision.*

Made in the USA
Middletown, DE
27 August 2022